Lean and Reorder Point Planning: Implementing the Approach the Right Way in Software

Shaun Snapp

Contents

CHAPTER 1

Introduction

MRP stands for materials requirements planning.

> *"Material requirements planning software (MRP) is*
> *used to describe the process of planning manufacturing*
> *inventory – what products to make and what items to buy,*
> *when, how much, and from whom – all based on supply*
> *and demand."*
>
> – What is MRP Software

1

MRP is one of the most important methods in supply chain planning. In performing research for this book, I found that MRP is the most commonly used term in supply chain planning, the next closest one being inventory management. This is true even though MRP is an old planning method for which many more advanced methods of planning have been developed. However, MRP (and DRP), while old, are still the most common methods of performing supply and production planning.

Interestingly, MRP is a much more commonly used term than DRP, or distribution resource planning, which is almost always used in conjunction with MRP and is the other topic of this book. In most instances, when a company talks about their MRP system, they actually mean their MRP/DRP system. But while both methods are used, I will be focusing on MRP for this book.

MRP is a procedure for **calculating dependent requirements** based upon a bill of materials, working backwards from the demand (also called independent requirements) of a forecasted item (MRP is emphatically a forecast-based planning method), along with sales orders which, when combined with lead-times, creates a series to planned production orders and purchase requisitions which are all timed to allow the demand to be met. I will repeatedly refer to the term procedure or procedural planning to describe non-Lean and non-reorder point planning. MRP, heuristics, cost optimization are all examples of procedures used in supply and production planning.

MRP was developed in the 1960's in the US, and incorporated into software and rolled out to companies on a small scale in the 1970's in most developed countries, becoming a dominant method of supply and production planning in the 1980's. However, reorder point planning had been incorporated into software roughly 10 years prior to MRP applications being sold and used but, given the immaturity of computer systems in the 1960's, few companies actually used these reorder points systems.

Therefore, there was no significant period of computerized reorder point systems prior to MRP systems. MRP can be considered to be the first broadly used computerized procedure for supply and production planning. The actual full leveraging of MRP's capabilities change depending upon the company, with some companies still having problems properly using MRP, and with many companies applying MRP or other supply planning methods incorrectly, when Lean approaches would be more appropriate.

The Methods Available for Supply Planning

Before we get into how to use multiple supply planning methods, let's review the supply planning methods that are available. Now is also a good time to explain that this book covers multiple methods for either the S&OP and rough-cut capacity plan or the initial supply plan, but does not cover using multiple methods for the deployment plan or for the redeployment.

There is a reason for this: while S&OP, rough-cut capacity plan, and the initial supply plan use the same methods, only in rare instances would the deployment and redeployment plan use multiple methods. A brief explanation of the different supply planning threads is included below:

1. *S&OP & Rough-Cut Capacity Plan:* These long-range planning threads are generally not part of the live environment. They are used for analytical purposes rather than to drive recommendations to the ERP system.

2. *The Initial Supply Plan (performed by MRP in ERP systems):* Produces initial production and procurement plan. It is focused on bringing stock into the supply network, and in creating stock with planned production orders. It can also be called the master production schedule (MPS) if the initial supply plan is run under certain criteria.[1] http://www.scmfocus.com/supplyplanning/2011/10/02/the-four-factors- that-make-up-the-master-production-schedule/

3. *The Deployment Plan (performed by DRP in ERP systems):* Focused on

---

[1] The MPS is a curious entity. It is how the demand flows to supply planning. As pointed out by the book *Factory Physics*, it *"provides the quantity and the due dates for all parts that have independent demand."* As stated by the book *Orlicky's Material Requirements Planning 3rd Edition,* "The MPS expresses the overall plan of production." It is stated in terms of end items, which may be either shippable products or highest-level assemblies from which these products are eventually built in various configurations according to a final assembly schedule. The MRP system "believes" the MPS, and the validity of its output is always relative to the contents of that schedule.

pushing stock from locations at the beginning of the supply network to the end of the supply network.

4. *The Redeployment Plan (performed by specialized applications with redeployment functionality or with a custom report):* Focused on repositioning stock which is already in the supply network to locations where it has a higher probability of consumption.

MRP is one of the best-known supply planning methods, but MRP only addresses the **initial supply plan**. The deployment plan is not created by MRP, but by a related procedure called DRP that was developed around 15 years after MRP. When MRP systems were first introduced, DRP had not yet been invented, so reorder point planning was used to trigger deployment.

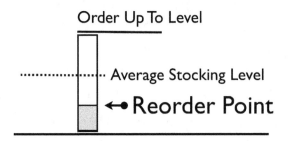

Reorder points are probably the easiest planning method to understand. They are often based upon an economic order quantity, which determines the batch size (or instead can be based upon the minimum order quantity). From there, reorder point is calculated, which accounts for the typical demand as well as the average lead-time.[2]

---

[2]   A very easy to use and convenient dynamic reorder point calculator is available at the following link: http://www.scmfocus.com/supplyplanning/2014/04/09/dynamic-reorder-point-calculator/

The MPS is normally a specific planning run in the supply planning application. The MPS is confusing because it has several different incarnations. When it is in the supply planning system, it is relatively easy to understand. However, as pointed out by Smith and Ptak, *"On occasion it has been suggested that the MPS, that is, its preparation and maintenance, could be automated and brought under complete computer control. This is envisioned as an extension of the process of automating systems and procedures in the area of manufacturing logistics.*

Prior to the development of procedural supply planning systems, reorder points were commonly used for the deployment. Different methods can be used for the initial supply plan and the deployment plan.

Books and Other Publications on Lean Reorder Points

As with all my books, I performed a comprehensive literature review before I began writing. One of my favorite quotations about research is from the highly respected RAND Corporation, a "think tank" based in sunny Santa Monica, CA. They are located not far from where I grew up. On my lost surfing weekends during high school, I used to walk right by their offices with my friend — at that time having no idea of the institution's historical significance. RAND's *Standards for High Quality Research and Analysis* publication makes the following statement about how its research references other work.

> *"A high-quality study cannot be done in intellectual isolation:*
> *It necessarily builds on and contributes to a body of research*
> *and analysis. The relationships between a given study and*
> *its predecessors should be rich and explicit. The study team's*
> *understanding of past research should be evident in many aspects*
> *of its work, from the way in which the problem is formulated and*
> *approached to the discussion of the findings and their implications.*
> *The team should take particular care to explain the ways in which*

Where statistical forecasting of demand applies, so the reasoning goes, the automated forecasting procedures could be integrated into a program of MPS calculation, including preparation of the schedule of factory requirements, netting product lot sizing and so on. The logic of the procedures can be clearly defined, and all the required data is available.

This notion must be repudiated. All the required data is, as a matter of fact, not available. Information on a multitude of extraneous factors, current company policy and seasoned managerial judgment - all of them bearing on the contents of an MPS - cannot be captured by the system. This is why management should be involved in the creation and maintenance of the MPS every step of the way."

What this means is that when companies have been calling their system run MPS without extracting it and interacting with it, they have been not performing their MPS properly. Because MPS is its own detailed topic and I wanted this book to be about improving MRP, I will not spend much time covering the MPS.

its study agrees, disagrees, or otherwise differs importantly from previous studies. Failure to demonstrate an understanding of previous research lowers the perceived quality of a study, despite any other good characteristics it may possess."

There are very few books that cover reorder points. I am not sure why this is, but I have an inkling that it is because reorder points are considered passé. Reorder points are covered in many supply chain books, but it is almost always from a high level, with most stopping at simply explaining the reorder point calculation. However, on the other hand, there seem to be an innumerable number of books on Lean.

I find it strange how Lean could be considered a "hot" topic while reorder points would be considered passé, because reorder points are one of the dominant methods within the Lean toolkit. For some reason, Lean books tend to be promotional in nature. There are a number of consultants who work in Lean and clearly many of these books are designed to help increase their consulting business.

In terms of the academic literature, there is quite a bit on the topic of reorder points, with older publications providing a more basic reorder point coverage, and with more modern publications providing quite esoteric reorder points calculations.[3]

One of the lesser-known facts is how complex reorder points can be, something I discuss specifically in *Chapter 2: The Lean Versus MRP Debate.*

1. *Improvement Oriented:* The book is focused on improving the common problems with MRP systems rather than explaining MRP.

2. *Software Focus*: This book will cover MRP conceptually, but this is about getting MRP **software** to work better.

---

[3] There are now books on Lean IT (information technology), Lean analytics and Lean startups. I am not sure what is next - Lean banking perhaps?

3. *Advancement Level*: This book is towards the advanced end of the spectrum.

4. *Non-Promotional*: Many books on a method like MRP are focused on promoting MRP versus other methods. This book does not do that. MRP has advantages and disadvantages over comparative methods, but this book does not spent time trying to convince companies to use any one particular deployment method. My other book, *MRP and DRP, Supply Planning with MRP, DRP and APS Software,* does provide an overall comparison of each of the supply and production planning methods.

The Use of Screen Shots in the Book

I consult in some popular and well-known applications, and I've found that companies have often been given the wrong impression of an application's capabilities. As part of my consulting work, I am required to present the results of testing and research about various applications. The research may show that a well-known application is not able to perform some functionality well enough to be used by a company, and point to a lesser-known application where this functionality is easily performed. Because I am routinely in this situation, I am asked to provide evidence of the testing results within applications, and screen shots provide this necessary evidence.

Furthermore, some time ago it became a habit for me to include extensive screen shots in most of my project documentation. A screen shot does not, of course, guarantee that a particular functionality works, but it is the best that can be done in a document format. Everything in this book exists in one application or another, and nothing described in this book is hypothetical.

Timing Field Definitions Identification

This book is filled with lists. Some of these lists are field definitions. The way to quickly identify which lists are field definitions is that they will be all *italicized*, while lists that are not field definitions will be only *italicized* for the term defined, while the definition that follows is not in normal text.

How Writing Bias Is Controlled at SCM Focus and SCM Focus Press

Bias is a serious problem in the enterprise software field. Large vendors receive uncritical coverage of their products, and large consulting companies recommend the large vendors that have the resources to hire and pay consultants rather than the vendors with the best software for the client's needs.

At SCM Focus, we have yet to financially benefit from a company's decision to buy an application showcased in print, either in a book or on the SCM Focus website. This may change in the future as SCM Focus grows – but we have been writing with a strong viewpoint for years without coming into any conflicts of interest. SCM Focus has the most stringent rules related to controlling bias and restricting commercial influence of any information provider. These "writing rules" are provided in the link below:

http://www.scmfocus.com/writing-rules/

If other information providers followed these rules, we would be able to learn about software without being required to perform our own research and testing for every topic.

Information about enterprise supply chain planning software can be found on the internet, but this information is primarily promotional or written at such a high level that none of the important details or limitations of the application are exposed; this is true of books on the subject as well.

When only one enterprise software application is covered in a book, one will find that the application works perfectly and operates as expected, and there are no problems during the implementation to bring the application live. This is all quite amazing and quite different from my experience of implementing enterprise software.

However, it is very difficult to make a living by providing objective information about enterprise supply chain software, especially as it means being critical at some point. I once remarked to a friend that SCM Focus had very little competition in providing untarnished information on this software category, and he said, "Of course, there is no money in it."

The Approach to the Book

By writing this book, I wanted to help people get exactly the information they need without having to read a lengthy volume. The approach to the book is essentially the same as with my previous books, and in writing this book I followed the same principles.

1. **Be direct and concise.** There is very little theory in this book, and the math that I cover is simple. While the mathematics behind the optimization methods for supply and production planning is involved, there are plenty of books which cover this topic. This book is focused on software, and for most users and implementers of the software, the most important thing to understand is conceptually what the software is doing.

2. **Based on project experience.** Nothing in the book is hypothetical; I have worked with it or tested it on an actual project. My project experience has led to me understanding a number of things that are not covered in typical supply planning books. In this book, I pass on this understanding to you.

3. **Saturate the book with graphics.** Roughly two-thirds of a human's sensory input is visual, and books that do not use graphics, especially educational and training books such as this one, can fall short of their purpose. Graphics have also been used consistently and extensively on the SCM Focus website.

The SCM Focus Site

As I am also the author of the SCM Focus site, http://www.scmfocus.com, the site and the book share a number of concepts and graphics. Furthermore, this book contains many links to articles on the site, which provide more detail on specific subjects. This book provides an explanation of how supply and production planning software works and aims to continue to be a reference after its initial reading. However, if your interest in supply planning software continues to grow, the SCM Focus site is a good resource to which articles are continually added.

The SCM site dedicated specifically to supply planning is http://www.scmfocus. com/supplyplanning

Intended Audience

This book is for anyone interested in better understanding Lean and reorder points, particularly from a detailed perspective of how to implement these approaches in systems. Many books cover reorder points from a mechanistic perspective and Lean from a philosophical perspective. This book describes practically how to apply these Lean and reorder points. The book is therefore targeted both to the doers as well as decision makers. I believe there is enough in the book to appeal to both types of audiences.

Abbreviations

A listing of all abbreviations used throughout the book is provided at the end of the book.

Corrections

Corrections and updates, as well as reader comments, can be viewed in the comment section of this book's web page. If you have comments or questions, please add them to the following link:

http://www.scmfocus.com/scmfocuspress/production-books/lean-and-reorder-points/

CHAPTER 2

The Lean versus MRP Debate

The Lean versus MRP debate (which I use as shorthand, as it is actually the Lean versus procedural debate, with MRP being just one – albeit the best known of the procedures that can be used for supply and production planning) is one of the most contentious in supply chain planning. Lean is actually a number of techniques, with reorder points being just one of them.

However, a major difference between Lean and MRP, or more accurately Lean versus procedural-based supply and production planning, primarily has to do with the replenishment trigger. Supply and production planning procedures such as MRP, heuristics, allocation, cost optimization, and inventory optimization work off projections, while Lean replenishment works off an immediate need.

Reorder point can be calculated a number of ways; for instance, it can be calculated differently based upon whether the **demand history is lumpy or stable**. Lean proponents generally want lower reorder quantities, more frequent ordering, and thus shorter durations between orders. This, of course, results in higher ordering, handling, and transportation costs.

Lean advocates tend to emphasize the costs of carrying and managing inventory, and tend to de-emphasize the other costs that inventories are put in place to
help minimize, namely manufacturing change-over costs, transportation costs,
and stock-out costs. This is a major issue and why I diverge from the more
extreme proponents of Lean is that they most frequently don't even mention
these costs, which will invariably rise.

Lean proponents propose that inventories cause inefficiencies that cannot necessarily be quantified. One of the common graphics they show is a basin filled
with liquid, with the liquid representing inventory. Within the basin are a series of problems, but unless the liquid, i.e. inventory, is drained, the problems
are not visible. While this is an interesting metaphor, but it cannot be considered proof of any particular inventory policy.

For instance, one could question how solvable the "problems" actually are, and
how unknown the problem actually is. For instance, if the problem is that the company has a shorter replenishment lead-time than customer lead-time, inventory is
a good way to solve this problem. This overall metaphor highlights a general criticism of Lean, which is brought up by the book *Factory Physics*, that Lean sometimes appears to be more of a philosophy than a science.[1] The following quotation
is a good synopsis of the criticisms of Lean.

---

[1] Lean has been called a cargo cult science. This term was developed by Richard Feyman,
a scientist who seems to pop up repeatedly both in his area of physics as well as other
disciplines. It refers to cultures – some of which were Pacific Island societies which
witnessed the great amount of material in the hands of the US military during the war
with Japan, and which attempted to replicate this surplus by building mock aircraft and
landing strips after the US military pulled out of these islands after WWII.

This is, of course, heavy criticism. Because of the wide variety of Lean proponents, books
on Lean and so on, it probably does apply to portions of Lean, but not necessarily to all
of it. Reorder points, for instance, are very well established to work well and could not be
considered part of any cargo cult science. However, there are quite a few proposals made
by Lean that don't have any evidence to support them aside from anecdotes, which could
be influenced by factors outside of the Lean approach being recommended. For instance,
the example of Japan having cultural advantages in terms of how they as a culture value attention to detail would be an example of one of these co-factors.

"Many Lean implementations attempt to abandon MRP. This causes tremendous friction between planning personnel and those pushing for that abandonment. Lean facilitators see MRP as an overly complex and wasteful dinosaur that simply does not work in the demand-driven world.

Planning personnel, however, see it in a completely different way. They understand that without the ability to see the total requirements picture, critical blind spots exist in the planning process that lead to shortages and/or even excessive inventory positions. They see the Lean approach as a gross oversimplification of the complex scenarios. MRP advocates desire a solution that identifies and manages the inherent dependencies in manufacturing situations. Most people in manufacturing don't even fully understand what the planning system is or does. Furthermore, "fixing" the system seems to be a never-ending intricate and expensive journey."

— Orlicky's Material Requirements Planning 3rd Edition

Lean adherents essentially propose that the standard mathematics of everything from the standard supply and production planning methods to Economic Order Quantity are incorrect and can be improved upon by reducing order quantities.[2] They propose that while the theory behind the calculations for supply and production planning methods as well as order batching might sound good, they don't work very well in reality.[3]

---

[2] The competition for setting manufacturing and inventory strategy is fierce. This is explained well in this quotation from *Factory Physics.* *"Lean, Six Sigma and SCM are each being sold as the solution to productivity problems in both manufacturing and services, as well as in other sectors such as construction and health care. The resulting competition between different approaches has fostered excessive zeal on the part of their proponents. But, as history has shown repeatedly, excessive zeal tends to result in programs being oversold to the point at which they degenerate into meaningless buzzwords. The periodic tendency of these trends to descend into marketing hype is one sign that there is a problem in the state of manufacturing management. The separation of the three trends into competing systems is a state of affairs that keeps good ideas from being disseminated."*

[3] There is a strong philosophical difference between Lean and planning orientations. While planning is much more about accepting the limitations and the system, Lean is much more about attempting to improve the constraints of the system.

Lean proponents are greatly assisted in their proposal by the poor quality of so many supply chain implementations that use procedures. I have been writing about the poor state of supply and production planning implementations for some time. However, there is really little financial incentive to improve this situation – in fact the financial incentives work in the opposite direction. This is why it's rare for information about supply chain - or other types of software implementations - to get out, unless there is a lawsuit and court documents are created.

It is well recognized that the way that MRP and other supply and production planning software are implemented and run in most companies leaves a significant opportunity for improvement. This is the conclusion of many of those who work in and have published in this area, and is my conclusion as well.

I cover both the common problems with MRP as well as the effective ways to improve MRP systems in the SCM Focus Press book *Repairing Your MRP System*. Furthermore, MRP is the easiest of the supply and production planning methods to master, with the more complex methods are more challenging to implement properly than MRP/DRP. There are really all sorts of reasons for this. I don't want to detract from what "is" rather than what "could be", but I consider most of the large consulting companies poor performers in terms of implementing the systems that use these methods. I often repair these applications post go-live and I routinely find very poorly configured systems.

Secondly, implementing companies tend to under-invest in the maintenance of these applications. Conversely, they often **over-invest** in the implementation. This is partially driven by promises of easy gains on the part of both software vendors and consulting companies, leaving them without the appropriate funding to maintain the system at the proper level.

I have documented the high maintenance costs of the enterprise software at the estimation site Software Decisions, and my research and estimates into this area show, on average, that the software acquisition costs only average roughly 10% of the total cost of ownership ("TCO"), and the majority of costs are found in maintenance. Still, neither software vendors, consulting companies, or IT analysts focus on TCO, and buyers/implementing companies continue to focus on enterprise software acquisition costs rather than the TCO of the software they purchase.

This topic is a lengthy discussion in its own right; however, the main take-away is that Lean proponents are correct when they say that many procedural planning systems have too much overhead and often do not meet the pre-implementation expectations.

In terms of analyzing their more tactical proposals, they are partially explained by the graph below:

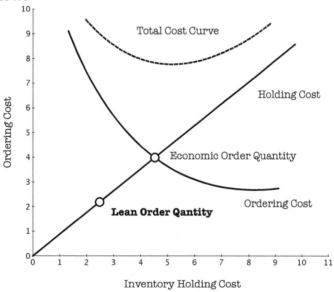

Lean proposes that smaller and more frequent orders are better for the overall supply chain. Lean is thus a contrarian philosophy to classical inventory management.

Are Reorder Points Always Simplistic?

Procedural supply planning proponents counter that Lean techniques are too simple and lack visibility. However, if we take the example of the reorder point, there are actually a variety of methods for calculating it. Reorder point planning is generally considered overly simplistic; however, this viewpoint misses the fact that reorder points **can be** set either very simply or in a complex fashion which is highly customized per product location. The paper, *"Determining Reorder Points When Demand is Lumpy,"* is a good example of this.

As an example of how complex reorder points can be, a few assumptions from this paper are as follows:

- A compound Poisson probability distribution is used. (A probability distribution specifically for lumpy or erratic demand. There are other papers, which use the negative binomial distribution, which is for extremely lumpy demand.)

- Lead-time is assumed to be known and constant.

- An assigned service level is assumed based upon a fraction of demand supplied without backorder.

- Joint optimization of order quantity and order point is not addressed, but rather order point is based on an independently calculated order quantity.

- Forecasting methods are not addressed, but the mean and variance of lead-time demand are assumed available.

- Further on in this chapter, I have listed quotations on reorder point planning that state that reorder point planning is only appropriate for products with a stable demand history; however, as can be seen above, this depends upon the method which is used to calculate the reorder point, and there are a wide variety of methods to choose from.

As with any other planning parameter, a reorder point must be reviewed with a frequency that matches the changes in the business. Writing this, I do not want to present a perfect world scenario as is commonly done in many books. I certainly know that any reorder point calculation will be updated much less frequently than it should be; however, that is true of all planning parameters, as it is true of lead time and other master data elements in supply planning.

Academic Versus Practitioner Views on Reorder Point Planning

There is an interesting dichotomy in the literature on reorder point planning. While mostly criticized in books written by practitioners, academic papers are filled with nuanced techniques for setting reorder points. The criticism by supply chain practitioners will often point out how unsophisticated reorder point planning is; however, reorder points can be set by either simple methods or by complex methods. Numerous academic papers that describe complex methods of reorder point determination demonstrate this fact. However, these sophisticated techniques for reorder point setting very **rarely** make their way to industry. Therefore, there is not a large demand for sophisticated reorder point setting because reorder point planning is rarely used. However, simply saying that reorder point planning is unsophisticated is not up to date with the scholarship on the topic.

Conclusion

If you come out of this chapter confused as to which side has the better points, I consider my job well done. As I will explain further on in this book, there is really no need to choose one or the other approach. In fact, much of the strong views on each side have more to do with maximizing billing hours and improving careers than what the actual evidence supports. Both procedures and Lean approaches can be used to good effect and they can be used within the same supply planning and production planning system.

I can say that there are two groups that don't have much of a leg to stand on in this debate, and these are the proponents on the extreme side of the debate that propose that Lean techniques should never be applied or, conversely, that only procedures should be used. I am in good a position to say this because I have tested all of the supply planning methods and all of the Lean techniques in multiple systems in real world environments. In fact, my proposal is that the strongest system actually leverages **both** schools of thought. The trick is determining which segments of the product location database should go out on which school of thought. I cover this in detail in *Chapter 8, Determining When to Use Lean Versus MRP.*

CHAPTER 3

Where Supply Planning Fits Within The Supply Plan

To begin, it is important to understand how the supply planning methods covered in this book relate within the overall context of enterprise supply chain software. The following mind map shows this relationship.

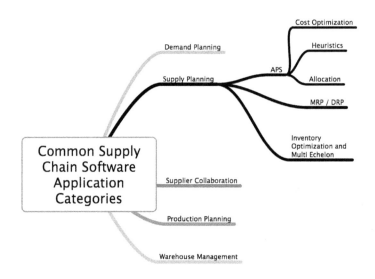

I list supply planning as the second supply chain software category because it immediately follows demand planning as a supply chain planning process. Although demand planning's forecasts are used by many processes, including S&OP, the main customer for demand planning forecasts is supply planning. Supplier collaboration integrates with supply planning and uses its planned on-hand stocking data. Product planning also uses data from the supply plan, developing production orders based on the supply plan. Warehouse management indirectly interacts with the supply plan; however, warehouse management systems are more strongly connected to the materials management function of the ERP system than to the supply planning system.

The graphic above does not fully explore the different subcategories within the major categories. For instance, Advanced Planning and Scheduling (APS) solutions also cover demand planning and supplier collaboration, but the purpose of this graphic is to describe APS only as it pertains to supply planning.

As you can see, APS is a catchall term that describes three different supply planning methods. MRP and DRP are listed together because they are closely related, with DRP essentially being an extension of MRP, but for outbound movements from the factory rather than inbound movements to the factory. MRP and DRP are normally part of the ERP system; however, they can also be located in external planning systems. For instance, SAP APO's PP/DS module has several heuristics that emulate MRP. In another example, Demand Works Smoothie, an external planning system, performs both MRP and DRP.

The Basic Nature of the Supply Chain Planning Functionality in ERP Systems

When I first began working with SAP ERP, I was extremely surprised at the limited functionality the application contained for supply chain planning. However, what I did not understand at the time was that most deep supply chain capabilities were not the focus of ERP systems. Instead, they put far more development emphasis into things such as finance and accounting, sales order management, and other operational functions than into supply chain planning. What made these systems popular was their supply chain functionality, which although basic, was integrated with finance, HR, etc. And although there have been some improvements since I worked in ERP, to this day, advanced supply chain functionality primarily resides outside ERP systems.

How ERP and APS Share the Planning Work

APS and ERP-based MRP work together on projects as a normal method of implementation. The most common approach has been for a company to implement one of the APS methods and then to use MRP in the ERP system to perform the bill of material (BOM) explosion. Under this design DRP in the ERP system is minimized as it is only used for the deployment of noncritical parts.

Critical versus Non-critical Materials

In MRP, the product database is often segmented into critical and noncritical materials, as described below.

- Critical materials, typically strategic, have longer lead times or are constrained by capacity.

- Noncritical materials are not restricted or difficult to obtain. As such, there is no compelling reason to put very much effort into planning noncritical materials.

After the critical materials have been identified, they are brought over from the ERP system to the external APS system (which resides on different hardware than the ERP system). Under this design, the APS system could apply any of its methods to the critical materials. The following options are possible:

- APS could apply its methods to just the finished goods, while the ERP system would perform all planning for the subcomponents.

• The APS system could apply its methods to both the finished goods and to the subcomponents.

Dependent Demand Products

Secondly, while dependent demand products such as subcomponents may make up a great deal of the products to be planned, they do not necessarily need to be forecasted or have advanced supply planning methods applied to them, as their procurement and deployment is entirely dependent upon the manufactured product and they are simply part of the BOM. Therefore, dependent demand products do not necessarily have to exist in external supply or demand planning systems. The MRP function of "exploding" the BOM and the creation of dependent demand procurement requisitions can occur in the ERP system after all demand and supply-planning activities have been performed in external planning systems. The supply planning system then applies the selected method on these critical and independent demand products (those that have demand directly forecasted for them and which have their own BOM). Once the plan is complete, the transaction recommendations (planned purchase orders, planned stock transfer orders, planned repair orders, and planned production orders—all of which can also be called either "planned orders" or "requisitions" as both terms are equally accurate) are sent to the ERP system for execution. To develop dependent requirements for subcomponents and to calculate independent and dependent requirements for noncritical materials that are also not planned in the APS, MRP is run in ERP, which explodes the BOM (extensively covered in the SCM Focus Press book *Supply Planning with MRP/ DRP and APS Software*, while BOM explosion is covered in Chapter 5: "MRP Explained"). If noncritical products are kept outside of the external planning system, as per the design above, then DRP is necessary in the ERP system to move these noncritical products, as they have not been planned in the APS system through the supply network.

This is commonly how MRP and DRP (supply planning methods that reside in one system: ERP) interact with the APS supply planning methods (heuristics, allocation, cost optimization), which are applied against products in another system.

Alternative Design

However, the design described above is not the only design. A second design plans both critical and noncritical products in the APS system, but not subcomponents. Under this design, MRP is still used to explode the BOM and create order requisitions for subcomponent procurement, but DRP is not required because the deployment of the noncritical products is managed by the external planning system. An additional point is that MRP is not the only mechanism within most ERP systems to perform BOM explosion. For instance in SAP ERP, the XO MRP Type's definition is "W/O MRP, with BOM Explosion." Therefore, while MRP is the most common way of exploding the BOM in ERP systems, it is not the only method available.

A third design is to plan all critical and noncritical products and subcomponents in the APS system and then to send the transaction recommendations over to the ERP system to perform execution only. In this case neither MRP nor DRP is required to be run in the ERP system because all the planning for all the products and all subcomponents has already been performed in the APS system. Specifically, the BOM has already been exploded, and the subcomponent (dependent demand) procurement recommendations and the deployment plan / stock transport requisitions for noncritical products have already been created.

Where a Product Location Combination is "Planned"

Some of the examples above demonstrate why it's important to add more specifics to the term "planned." Unfortunately it is very easy to fall into the habit of saying that a product is planned in one system or another, when in fact we generally speak of a product being planned in one system only. For instance, the most common distinction is the one made above where critical products are *planned entirely* in the SAP APO application versus noncritical products being *planned entirely* (usually with MRP) in the ERP system. Under this design, the delineation between being "planned" in one system or another is very clear. However, this distinction becomes less clear when one of the planning stages is performed in one system and a second in another. This is because "planned in" is not a sufficiently detailed description to explain what is happening and where it is happening. A product can have the finished good planning performed in APO, with the subcomponents planned either with MRP or with simple BOM explosion. For products with multiple nesting in their bill of material, the finished good could be planned in APO, with the semi-finished good and raw material planned in R/3. Alternatively, both the finished good and semi-finished good could be planned in APO, and only the raw material planned in R/3.

Conclusion

Supply planning software sits between demand planning and applications such as supplier collaboration and production planning. It is often considered the intersection point or heart of the supply chain planning process because it interacts with all the other major planning components. Supply planning systems can perform first-cut production planning by incorporating production batch sizes and production capacity constraints into the supply planning system.

All supply planning is performed by no more than six methods (the sixth being inventory optimization and multi-echelon planning) by all companies globally. However, because MRP is not a complete supply planning method without DRP, the methods can be counted in two different ways. Therefore I often combine MRP/DRP into one method, which would make for only five methods. In order for a method to be complete it must address both the initial plan and the deployment plan. The initial plan (or network plan as it is sometimes called) is the production and procurement plan, while the deployment plan creates stock transfer recommendations between the supply network locations. All the other methods (not MRP and DRP) can be used for either the initial supply plan or for the deployment plan. However, they do so with different parameters in place. Therefore, the configuration for cost optimization or allocation (often stored in some type of profile) for deployment is a completely separate configuration from the allocation or cost optimization that controls the initial or network plan. MRP and DRP are the only methods that perform "one half" of the supply planning process only. Therefore while they are broadly known as two different things, they can be thought of as complementary parts of one method.

MRP/DRP is normally run from an ERP system but it can also be performed in APS systems. One supply planning application called Demand Works Smoothie performs MRP/DRP but is neither an APS system nor an ERP system. APS supply planning methods are usually co-implemented with MRP/DRP functionality in order to develop a supply plan for both critical and noncritical materials, and three different designs for accomplishing this have been listed and are generally well known. Most likely more designs exist, as it is difficult to guess all the ways that companies have decided to connect their external supply planning systems to their ERP systems.

CHAPTER 4

Reorder Point Planning

Reorder point planning was the primary way that supply chain planning was performed before computers existed. Reorder point planning was at first performed manually and, just prior to the arrival of MRP systems, reorder point planning software was commercialized in mainframe computers in the 1950's and 1960's in the United States. This is why inventory systems were not perpetual or instantly updated when, for instance, the actual inventory changed, because each reorder point had to be recalculated by hand; therefore each product location combination was set onto a different review periodicity.

After MRP was first developed in the 1960's and broadly implemented in the late 1970's, companies moved away from reorder point planning, and reorder point planning was relegated to a lower status vis-à-vis MRP/DRP. Again reorder point planning was soon considered passé. Of course, much of the reason for this was that MRP/DRP software vendors said that reorder points were passé and most of the consulting companies that were obtaining an increasing percentage of their consulting revenues from MRP/DRP software implementations **naturally** agreed with them.

The concept since this time has generally been that all products should have a supply planning method applied to them rather than use reorder points. In a few paragraphs, I will discuss why this is incorrect, and why proponents of "Lean" have caught on to something which is correct with respect to reorder point planning which many experts in supply planning are missing. I consider this explanation important, because individuals that recommend reorder point planning for some items tend to meet stiff resistance from those of an MRP bent; however, much of this resistance is due to not properly considering the conditions under which reorder point planning is effective.

Reorder Points in Their Essence
A reorder point is very simply a quantity of stock or an interval at which a "reorder," or order, is to be created. In reorder point planning, orders are not triggered by a specific requirement (such as a forecast or dependent requirement), but instead by the depletion of stock over time, eventually triggering the minimum stock level or reorder point. Production orders, purchase orders, and stock transfer orders are generated based upon the relationship between the stocking level and the reorder point. This is stated by SAP in their application help:

> *"Available stock at plant level plus the firmed receipts that have already been planned (purchase orders, production orders, firmed purchase requisitions and so on) are compared with the reorder point. If the sum of the stock plus receipts is less than the reorder point, a material shortage exists."*

Reorder points can be used with any of the supply planning methods, or they can be used to exclusively control the supply plan **without any of the methods**. However, when they are used exclusively to control the supply plan, the company is **said to be performing** reorder point planning, as opposed to forecast-based planning.

MRP/DRP and APS (heuristic, allocation, cost optimization, inventory optimization) methods are **forecast-based planning**. As the terminology would indicate, reorder point planning does not require a forecast. The following graphic shows how this works:

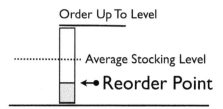

The reorder point is a calculated value, expressed as a stocking level, which is then implemented in a supply planning system and stored as a master data parameter. If a company had 100 products, all of which had a reorder point entered in the product location master, and 50 were excluded from the supply planning run – let's say the MRP run, then 50 of the product locations would be using the MRP supply planning method, and the other 50 would be on reorder point planning. Therefore, a reorder point can be used with or without a specific supply planning method.

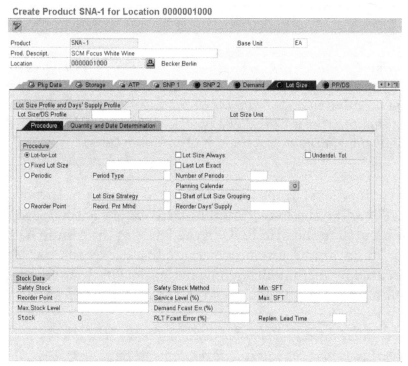

This is the Lot Size tab to the product location master in SAP APO/SCM. As can be seen, there are not a lot of alternatives provided here, just the basics. The reason for this is these reorder points are not designed to actually control the planning (that is supposed to be performed by heuristics, the optimizer, or CTM.), but instead these order points are used to moderate the order creation in APO.

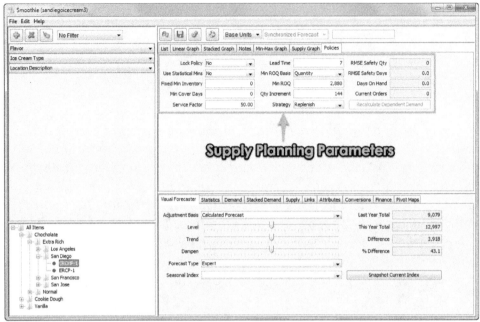

In the application Demand Works Smoothie, the inventory parameters are very concentrated onto a single tab. Important fields that relate to reorder point planning are the Fixed Minimum Inventory, Minimum Reorder Quantity (Min ROQ), the Minimum Reorder Quantity Basis (Min ROQ Basis), the Quantity Increment (Qty Increment), as well as the Minimum Cover Days (Min Cover Days).

When the inventory level drops below the Fixed Minimum Inventory, an order is triggered. Therefore the Fixed Minimum Inventory is the reorder point. The order will be created in the Min ROQ in the UOM of the Min ROQ Basis (either a quantity or in days) and any order created that exceeds the Min ROQ will need to be created by incrementing upward in the Qty Increment. More on the Fixed Minimum Inventory is explained in the *Smoothie Help*:

> *"This is interpreted by Smoothie as the quantity that the inventory must not go below. Smoothie will recommend receipts to keep ending inventory above this amount (outside the supply fence) and report over/under conditions within the supply fence. The Fixed Min Inventory value drives the Minimum Inventory when the Use Statistical Mins selector is set to No. If the selector is on Linear (or Linear No Outliers), then the greater value (Fixed or RMSE Safety*

Qty) will be selected as the minimum inventory. Fixed Min Inventory is ignored if the Use Statistical Mins selector is set to Cover (or Cover No Outliers)."

In Smoothie, consumption-based replenishment can also be triggered by falling below the Min Cover Days. This simply allows the replenishment trigger to be stated in days rather than in a quantity. All of this brings up the topic of the economic order quantity, which goes hand in hand with the reorder point. Now is a good time to cover the economic order quantity (EOQ).

Introduction to Economic Order Quantity

The reorder point tells the system **when to** reorder, while the economic order quantity tells the system **how much** to order; as such they are necessarily highly integrated values.

EOQ is one method for performing what is generally known as lot sizing. The lot size is the quantity in which the item is produced or procured and therefore it is set at the production location combination in the product master. Here it is in *Demand Works Smoothie* on their Policies Tab.

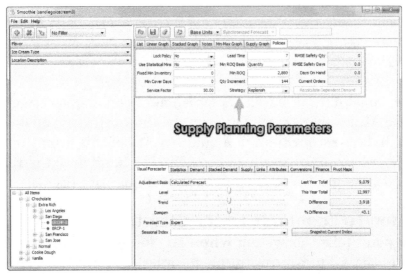

Here the fields the Min ROQ Base (Reorder Quantity) and the ROQ (Reorder Quantity) are the relevant fields. Here the Min ROQ states that one must order in a minimum quantity of 2,880 units. The Qty Increment of 144 units means that after the minimum is met, when more than the minimum is required, the item may be ordered in increments of 3,024, 3,168, 3,312, etc. The other alternative in this application is to set the Min ROQ Basis to Days, and in that case the Min ROQ and the Qty Increment would not reflect units, but would reflect days.

Common methods of calculating the lot size are the following:

1. *Lot for Lot*: This is confusingly named because lot for lot is simply a lot size based upon the net requirements in a particular period. Therefore it is essentially **no** lot size. Using lot for lot sizing would be considered Lean as the company is only producing or procuring what it absolutely knows that it needs.

2. *Economic Order Quantity*: This bases the lot size on a financial calculation.

3. *Periodic Order Quantity*: This is simply the economic order quantity, but stated in terms of a reorder frequency.

Economic order quantity is actually one of the oldest formulae in inventory management. The development of EOQ is, in my view, the most interesting story I can recall reading of all of the supply chain management calculations I have investigated.

EOQ was first developed by Ford W. Harris in 1913. As with the development of MRP, the originator of EOQ was not an academic. In fact, at the time he developed EOQ, he did not even have an undergraduate degree. EOQ has proven to be one of the most durable calculations in all of inventory management and has held up remarkably well.

Some have proposed that because EOQ does not automatically adjust with the variability of its inputs, it cannot be used for more product location combinations (PLC's) with more variable demand history, and this is true - if the data provided to the EOQ is not periodically changed. Therefore, it must be **periodically** recomputed for the entire product location database. It would be relatively easy to make the EOQ formula continuously altered based upon changes on its inputs, but I have yet to see this functionality in any supply planning application. I cover how to intelligently periodically update inventory parameter information in *Appendix B: Inventory Parameter Calculation with 3S*.

Validity and Applicability of EOQ

EOQ was original developed for a production lot sizing. However, the book *Factory Physics* states the following with respect to EOQ:

> *"For example, in 1913, Harris published his original EOQ paper and established a precise mathematical standard for efficiency research with his famous "square root formula" for the lot size problem. While elegant, this formula relied on assumptions that – for many real-world production systems – were highly questionable.*
>
> *1. A fixed, known setup cost*
> *2. Constant deterministic demand*
> *3. Instantaneous delivery (infinite capacity)*
> *4. A single product or no product interactions*
>
> *Because of these assumptions, EOQ makes much more sense applied to purchasing environments than to the production environment for*

which Harris intended it. In a purchasing environment, setups (i.e. purchase orders) may adequately be characterized with constant costs. However in manufacturing systems, setup costs cause all kinds of other problems (e.g., product mix implications, capacity effects, variability effects). The assumptions of EOQ completely gloss over these important issues."

Using Economic Order Quantity in Systems

After EOQ's calculation, it is most often placed into the minimum order quantity field which all supply planning systems have. This sets the minimum order level. However, sometimes other factors that are larger than this - such as when products must be purchased in rail car loads, set the actual minimum order level. In that case, no EOQ calculation is necessary. The minimum order quantity is the carload.

While the formula is one of the easiest in supply chain to calculate, many companies do not determine their unconstrained products (that is unconstrained by minimum order sizes such as with the example of the car load, or minimum package quantities) on the basis of EOQ.

However, there really is no reason aside from work effort to not do so – and in fact, the work effort is quite low. For whatever reason, most companies don't get around to calculating EOQ or, if they do calculate it, they do so **very infrequently**.

Students at university are often told that EOQ is frequently used in industry, when in fact it isn't (this is just one of the misrepresentations of supply chain management on the part of college courses and supply chain textbooks). But this does not mean that it should not be used.

EOQ certainly adds value and quantifies and then trades off the most important costs for making an ordering decision. That is the truth of how understaffed supply chain management departments are. They often do not have the staffing to apply elementary inventory management techniques that **are over 80 years old**.

Economic Order Quantity and Forecast Error

The higher the forecast error, the less use the EOQ value is. This is because as the forecast error increases, the likelihood that the quantity will be consumed declines. However, this is no different from any other supply planning parameter; supply planning parameters have the highest value when the forecast is most accurate.

EOQ and Quantity Discounts

If there are quantity discounts, the calculation below will not be accurate. For instance, the formula below may propose an EOQ of 184 units. If the price per each at this level is $50, then this is a total cost of (184 * $50) + 45 or $9,245. However, if the quantity discount kicks in at 200 units and this discount is 15%, then 16 more units could be obtained for $8,538. This would be a missed opportunity.

This can be easily calculated for an individual item, but this cannot really be systematized because supply planning applications do not have EOQ functionality or even step function min lot sizes. Typically this is handled by procurement as they are up to date on the volume discounts and will increase the orders to meet the discount.

This is the very well-known sawtooth pattern, which is a feature of the stocking level rising to its highest point when a new procurement order is received or a new pro-

duction order is completed, and with the stocking level declining to its lowest point right before the procurement order is received or right before a new production order is scheduled. The minimum stock level should be the safety stock, which the inventory level may consume due to variability in demand or supply.

EOQ actually has a number of slight adjustments to the formula used to account for different requirements, like the calculator included at the link below which calculates an EOQ in the case where the company wants to build inventory.

http://www.scmfocus.com/supplyplanning/2014/04/20/economic-order-quantity-calculator-pull-forward-inventory-build/

EOQ and Perishability

There can be scenarios where the shelf life of the product does not allow for the full EOQ to be ordered. In this case, the EOQ formula should not be used, and the shelf life time, converted into units, should be used instead (Silver and Peterson).

The same issue applies to products that go through frequent revisions, where ordering the EOQ would or could result in significant obsolescence. EOQ must also be managed versus storage capacity. In general, storage capacity is less expensive than accepting increased costs through shorter production runs. However, this does not seem to have much influence with companies because they cannot quantify how their production costs change from changing the length of production runs.

Therefore, philosophy rather than facts tends to rule the day with a much greater focus being placed in inventory and storage costs rather than production costs. Although, this greatly depends upon the company. Some companies work exactly the opposite, focusing very little on reducing inventory and being primarily focused on minimizing procurement costs through buying in very large and uneconomic quantities. The question becomes quite a bit more grey for procured items where the costs to be traded off are quantity discounts and order costs.

EOQ and Production Planning

If the item in question is procured, then the standard term "ordering cost," which is often used with the EOQ formula, is correct. However, if the EOQ is being calculated for an internally produced item, then the order cost becomes the "ordering and setup/changeover cost."

This is the cost of changing the line over to a new product. This is because what is called the ordering cost is really just the total costs for initiating the replenishment. Unfortunately, few companies have realistic costings for their changeovers. Therefore, it usually takes some time to develop these costs.

Background on Reorder Point Planning in SAP

For many years, companies used reorder point planning in SAP ERP before some companies decided to move to APO for their planning. Reorder point planning is still quite popular with a number of companies. As I describe in the SCM Focus Press book *Supply Planning with MRP, DRP, and APS Software,* in a historical review of the topic of reorder point planning that was research for the book, I have concluded that reorder point planning has been unfairly maligned, primarily by software vendors and consultants and even a number of authors chose to take a one sided view of the topic, characterizing reorder point planning as passe.

Many of the arguments used against reorder point planning don't hold up under scrutiny when one considers products with certain demand history characteristics (I provide this scrutiny to specific anti-reorder point planning quotations taken from other books). I say this having worked in, and implemented, every supply planning method that is available in software: reorder points have their place, and many of the critics of reorder point planning have unfounded reasons for resisting them.

Reorder Point Planning in SAP ERP

Let's look at the reorder point controls that are found on the *Material Master* in SAP ERP. This is the most common ERP system, but most systems with supply planning functionality work in a similar manner. SAP has the following quotations on reorder points:

"The system then calculates the net requirements. The system compares the available stock at plant level (including safety stock) plus the firmed receipts that have already been planned (purchase orders, production orders, firmed purchase requisitions and so on) with the reorder point. If the sum of the stock plus receipts is less than the reorder point, a material shortage exists."

– SAP Help

This makes it sound as if the reorder point in SAP ERP does forward calculate, but an important question is for how long.

The reorder level (also known as the reorder point) is made up of the sum of the safety stock plus the expected average material consumption within the replenishment lead-time. Therefore, when determining the reorder level, you must take safety stock, previous consumption values or future requirements, and the replenishment lead time into account.

– SAP Help

Therefore, it is over the replenishment lead-time. So in a formula format, it looks like the following:

Sum (Safety Stock + Expected Average Consumption for the Replenishment Lead Time)

The reorder level or point is essentially the demand over lead-time + the safety stock, which is the upper level of demand based upon the variability in supply and demand (depending upon how the company calculates safety stock and what the safety stock takes into account).

Manual or Externally Calculated Reorder Point Planning in SAP ERP

Once the external program produces values, or if the reorder points are to be manually determined, these are the fields that are populated. This is shown in the following screen shot:

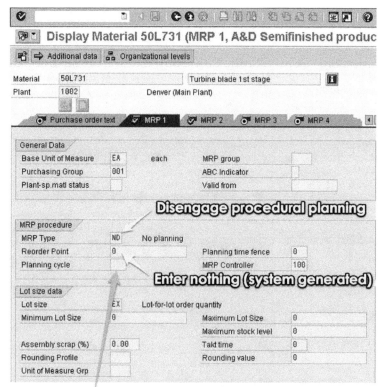

Automatic Reorder Point in SAP ERP

When calculated automatically using the base functionality in SAP ERP, SAP has the following quote on how this works:

> *"If you choose the automatic reorder point planning procedure then both the reorder level and the safety stock level are determined by the integrated forecasting program. The system determines the forecast values for future requirements by means of historical data. From these forecast values, the system then calculates the reorder level and the safety stock level, taking the service level, which is specified by the MRP controller, and the material's replenishment lead time into account. The system then records these two values in the appropriate material master record. Since the forecast is carried out at regular intervals, the reorder level and the safety stock level are continually*

adapted to the current consumption and delivery situation. This means that a contribution is made towards keeping stock levels low."
– SAP Help

This is shown in the graphic below:

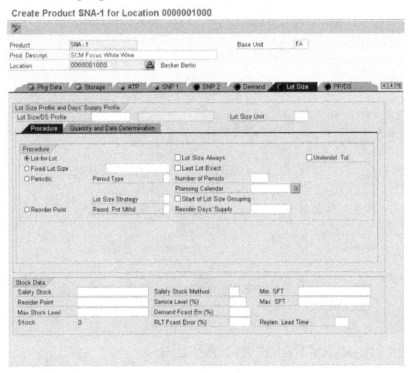

This setting would be a problem for many clients that I work with. They don't necessarily want their safety stock determined by an integrated forecasting program just because they are selecting automatic reorder point determination. Using this also means setting a service level and setting it for every product location combination. This can be another problem because companies typically don't have a custom service level, but often have blanked service levels. However, a blanked service level for large parts of the product database can be applied. Some schemes may look like the following:

1. A Products: 98% Service Level

2. B Products: 95% Service Level

3. C Products 88% Service Level

Once the external program produces values, or if the reorder points are to be manually determined, these are the fields that are populated. Setting service levels with safety stock in the most integrated and intelligent way that I am aware of, and the approach I recommend to all of my clients, is explained in the *Appendix B: Inventory Parameter Calculation with 3S*.

Conclusion

A reorder point is very simply a quantity of stock or an interval at which a "reorder," or order, is to be created. In reorder point planning, orders are not triggered by a specific requirement (such as a forecast or dependent requirement), but instead by the depletion of stock over time, eventually triggering the minimum stock level or reorder point. Reorder points can be used with any of the supply planning methods, or they can be used to exclusively control the supply plan **without any of the methods**. However, when it is used exclusively to control the supply plan, the company is **said to be performing** reorder point planning, as opposed to forecast-based planning. MRP/DRP and APS (heuristic, allocation, cost optimization, inventory optimization) methods are forecast-based planning.

CHAPTER 5

Lean Planning

Where Did Lean Come From?

The history of supply chain planning since roughly the 1970's has been a story of the development of increasingly sophisticated mathematics for performing planning. Then along came Lean, which called into question the applicability of these methods, and essentially proposed going back to the earlier simpler methods. It seems natural to question where this all came from. Interestingly, in terms of the origin of Lean, it came from the Toyota Production System, or TPS. However, the TPS drew parts of its approach from Ford Motor Company. This is explained in the following quotation, which is from the book *Today and Tomorrow*:

> "I was first introduced to the concepts of just-in-time (JIT) and the Toyota production system in 1980. Subsequently I had the opportunity to witness its actual application at Toyota on one of our numerous Japanese study missions. There I met Mr. Taiichi Ohno, the system's creator. When bombarded with questions from our group on what inspired his thinking, he just laughed and said he learned it all from Henry Ford's book. The scale, rigor

43

and continuous learning aspects of TPS have made it a core concept
of Lean."

Actually, this is an oversimplification because it is also well-known that the management at Toyota felt parts of Ford's manufacturing approach needed to be altered, so the TPS is better described as a combination of the Ford manufacturing approach with many cultural aspects that are specific to Japan. However, the degree of credit given by the main intellectual force behind the TPS, Taiichi Ohno, is quite remarkable:

> *"We have learned a lot from the US automotive empire. America has*
> *generated wonderful production management techniques, business*
> *management techniques such as quality control (QC), and total*
> *quality control (TQC), and industrial engineering (IE) methods.*
> *Japan imported these ideas and put them into practice. The Japanese*
> *should never forget that these techniques were born in America and*
> *generated by American efforts."*

In terms of why Lean is such a strong trend, in fact a trend that extends far beyond manufacturing, I believe that Lean has been driven in large part by dissatisfaction in the quality of the output from supply and production planning systems. This dissatisfaction can stem anywhere from MRP's logic being overly simplistic to where implementing companies have run into problems implementing supply planning methods more complex than MRP/DRP. However, it should also be noted that all of the methods employed in manufacturing and inventory management have been disappointing in one way or another for the majority of companies that implement them.

> *"Americans seem to have a stubborn faith in the eventual emergence*
> *of a swift and permanent solution to the manufacturing problem.*
> *Each successive approach to manufacturing management – scientific*
> *management, operations research, MRP, JIT, TQM, BPR, ERP,*
> *SCM, Lean, Six Sigma and so on have been sold as the solution.*
> *Each one has disappointed us, but we continue to look for the elusive*
> *"technology silver bullet" which will save American manufacturing."*
> — Factory Physics

The Big Lean Trend

Currently there is a great focus on the topic of Lean. While Lean is continually presented as fresh and new, in fact it has quite a long history – and I am not only speaking of its history at its point of origin, which is Japan.

Just in time inventory (JIT), which was one of the major pillars of the Toyota production system (or TPS for short) was extremely popular in the 1980's and was part of the Japanese manufacturing craze that affected pretty much all discrete manufacturers, and many types of manufacturing outside of discrete manufacturing to some degree or another.[1]

The book *Factory Physics* has the following comment on JIT:

> *"...MRP II was roundly criticized in the 1980's, while Japanese firms were strikingly successful by going back to methods resembling the old reorder point approaches. JIT advocates were quick to sound the death knell of MRP. But MRP did not die, largely because MRP II handled important non-production data maintenance and transaction processing functions, jobs that were not replaced by JIT."*

---

[1] I did find a different opinion of what manufacturing environments are suitable for JIT. This is explained in the following quotation from the book *Factory Physics*: *"A system in which discrete parts are produced at a fairly steady flow rate is called a repetitive manufacturing environment. The KANBAN system developed by Toyota...is best suited to repetitive manufacturing environments."*

The distinction between repetitive and discrete manufacturing environments is the rate of production and the frequency of changeovers. I do not consider automotive manufacturing repetitive because the manufacturing rate is too low. However, the distinction comes into effect with respect to what manufacturing process is being referred to. The simpler components and subcomponents can be produced on high speed lines – brakes, wheels, axles, etc. This is a repetitive manufacturing environment. However, more complex sub assemblies are not produced on high speed lines and this is discrete manufacturing.

Secondly, the assembly of the automobile is most definitely discrete manufacturing. Therefore, automobile manufacturing is an example of a mixed manufacturing environment. However, because the majority of the production is discrete, I believe it's most accurate to refer to it as discrete. Wikipedia categorizes automobile production as discrete as well.

It's well known that Lean is in part renamed and rebranded JIT. A cynical view of this renaming is that JIT lost much of its credibility in the marketplace and therefore a new term was used in order to improve acceptance. Like JIT, Lean is a philosophy that originated in manufacturers and then migrated over to supply planning. There are books that explain how to apply Lean to retailers and wholesale operations. Two of the most prominent ideas touted by Lean are listed below:

1. *Variability*: Lean holds that variability is the main problem in supply chains, and that management of variability should be a **main focus** of supply chain planning. This can entail either reducing the variability or placing buffers closest to the point of variability. (Reducing variability may mean switching to a more reliable transportation company that delivers consistently. Adding a buffer would mean keeping sufficient inventory at the receiving location to account for the inconsistency of the delivery company.)

2. *Not Forecasting:* Rather than performing forecasting, the supply chain should instead be reactive and only carry a minimal amount of inventory. This can be accomplished by reorder point planning, and minimal inventory can be achieved by how the reorder point (either duration or quantity) is set.

I want to be sure to address each of these Lean proposals, because to simply list the proposals of Lean without commenting on the history and feasibility would be a disservice to the reader.

1. *Safety Stock and Variability:* Systems with supply planning functionality account for variability with safety stock. This would work well, but most companies have such poor maintenance and such unsophisticated calculations of safety stock that they often use their safety stock ineffectively.[2]

   Some of the criticisms leveled by Lean proponents at safety stock have more to do with poor maintenance of safety stock and inappropriate cal-

---

[2] I cover this in the SCM Focus Press book *Safety Stock and Service Levels: A New Approach.*

culation of safety stock than how safety stock can be calculated. I am in complete agreement that safety stock as implemented has many problems within companies.

However, the issue with respect to variability is that proponents of Lean and the supply chain in general have very little control **over much** of its variability. This is because Sales and Marketing are constantly ratcheting up the number of products offered and which must therefore be manufactured.

Sales and Marketing generally do not worry about the pressure that this places on the supply chain. I find it strange that Lean proponents have taken such a narrow view of variability and have not been aggressive in admonishing Sales and Marketing to make the overall supply chain more sustainable by lowering product proliferation.

2. *The Feasibility of Not Forecasting:* This is not possible for most clients and in most situations. For this to work, the replenishment lead-time must the shorter than the lead-times between the customer's order and the expected delivery date. If most companies were to move away from forecasting and wait until sales orders arrive to engage in production or procurement, they would quickly lose a big component of their revenues.

Lean proponents who talk about a 100% pull system often give examples such as Dell – which for part of its business is an assemble-to-order operation, which means it forecasts at the component level (and then assembles-to-order when the configuration comes through on the sales order) - or they provide examples of make-to-order manufacturing environments.

This does not represent a very large percentage of the overall manufacturing market, so it seems strange and vaguely misleading to continually emphasize supply chain planning techniques that are designed for manufacturing environments that cannot be broadly applied.

For instance, the executive who works for a pen company is not going to be able to move his or her company to an make-to-order manufacturing environment because there is little demand and little willingness to pay the premium for custom pens.

Lean is all about reducing muda (non-value added activity), muri (overburden) and mura (unevenness) or, roughly speaking, all forms of waste. The areas of waste that Lean attempts to reduce are the following:

1. *Transport (moving products that are not actually required to perform the processing)*

2. *Inventory (all components, work in process and finished product not being processed)*

3. *Motion (people or equipment moving or walking more than is required to perform the processing)*

4. *Waiting (waiting for the next production step, interruptions of production during shift change)*

5. *Over-production (production ahead of demand)*

6. *Over-processing (resulting from poor tool or product design creating activity)*

7. *Defects (the effort involved in inspecting for and fixing defects)-*

There are many books and conferences dedicated to Lean, and perhaps you have already derived your own opinions as to what Lean is. There are also several different ways of practicing Lean, so it's difficult to say definitively how all its practitioners recommend using the philosophy.

Secondly, some corporate initiatives are called Lean, but are not in fact based upon Lean principles, further eroding the actual concept of Lean as it is generally understood. There are also examples of Lean being used as an excuse to push responsibility onto one's suppliers, as the article in the following link describes:

http://www.scmfocus.com/supplychaincollaboration/2012/02/lean-as-acover-story-by-oems-to-force-their-poor-planning-decisions-on-contractmanufacturers/

As I see it Lean, as applied to supply planning software, really boils down to several main thrusts:

1. The ability to collaborate with suppliers, thus increasing pipeline visibility in order to reduce the disintegration of order sequence that continues to mar the supply chain.

2. Reduce forecasting and specifically reduce the waste in the forecasting process.

3. Reduce the quantities ordered.

The Honesty of How Lean is Presented

There are significant discrepancies between how Lean is often presented and the reality of the history of Lean. Some of these discrepancies are the following:

1. *Lean's Cultural Implication*: One discussed feature of the TPS that surfaced during research for this book is that the TPS may simply be a better fit for Japanese culture.[3] Not only have other companies had a difficult time in faithfully implementing the TPS, but even Toyota has had a difficult time faithfully implementing its system in its factories **outside** of Japan. This is also left out of most books on the Lean topic. Obviously, it helps sell the concept better if it is through that "anyone" can implement the Toyota Production System.

   This is much like TV infomercials regarding exercise products. The benefits of the people in the advertisement are all attributed to something the viewer can buy. The effort level of the spokesperson, their lifetime of fitness background, their age, and the other things they might do to keep in shape outside of the exercise product being sold, are left out of the discussion.

---

[3] As pointed out in the book *Factory Physics*, "*The roots of JIT undoubtedly extend deep into Japanese cultural, geographic, and economic history. Because of their history of living with space and resource limitations, the Japanese are inclined towards conservation. Eastern culture is also more systems-oriented than Western culture with its reductionist scientific roots.*

Policies that cut across individual workstations, such as cross-trained floating workers and total quality management, are more natural in this environment. Geography has also certainly influenced Japanese practices. Policies involving delivery of materials from suppliers several times per day are simply easier in Japan where industry is spatially concentrated, than in America with wide open spaces."

If TPS is something that is particular to Japan's culture, then it's less appealing for broad consumption. This is the problem with so many books in business books fact; they are more interested in "pumping up" a particular approach than describing things accurately.

In fact, while Japan's quality in manufacturing items was highlighted in innumerable books in the 1980's and often attributed to various techniques that could, supposedly, be easily copied, if one goes back in history, Japan has for many hundreds of years produced extremely high quality goods. These were not made in mass production, because mass production did not exist prior to the Industrial Revolution, but in hand crafted products such as silk tapestries. During the colonial period, luxury Japanese-produced goods were fixtures in houses of wealthy Europeans.

2. *The Learning Aspect of the TPS*: Building on the cultural basis for the success of the TPS, the following quotation is instructive. "*It has been said that the typical US firm, when facing a vexing problem which it has one year to solve, would spend three months planning, three months implementing, six months tweaking and picking up loose ends.*

> "*Toyota facing a similar situation would spend eleven months planning and one month implementing (with no loose ends to clean up!).*" *This comparison is an exaggeration of course, but it nonetheless contains an important element of truth. The reason Toyota spends so much time and effort on the planning phase is because that phase is so important to learning.*

> "*Toyota managers want to make sure they deeply understand the background and the facts of the current situation before moving forward. After the current state is thoroughly probed, they want to establish with a high degree of certainty that they have accurately identified the root of the problem.*"
> – Understanding A3 Thinking: A Critical Component of
> Toyota's PDCA Management System.

Of course, any company that has employees that follow such an approach will have success with a variety of techniques. Hence the problem of differentiating the power of the specific technique versus the company's environment is a constant problem when attempting to analyze the TPS.

3. *Leaving Out Demand Shaping*: Lean is presented, or should I say tends to be presented as there are so many Lean proponents, as having all of the variability accounted for by the supply chain. However, that was not the original approach outlined by the TPS.

   As pointed out in the book, *Factory Physics*, *"Americans took due dates as exogenously provided and attempted to optimize the production schedule. The Japanese realized that due dates are negotiated with customers and worked to integrate marketing and manufacturing to provide production schedules that do not require precise optimization or abrupt changes."*

   This same issue has been misrepresented by Lean consultants that have promoted the Dell approach. But more broadly, Sales and Marketing could work to not simply sell everything, but to sell what is available. This part of what is referred to as demand shaping.[4]

---

[4] That is, at Dell, Sales and Marketing did not simply sell everything but made an effort to sell what was available. This is part of what is referred to as demand shaping. This is covered in the following quotation:

"Dell purposely selected customers with relatively predictable purchasing patterns and low service costs. The company developed a core competence in targeting customers, and kept a massive database for this purpose. A large portion of Dell's business stemmed from long-term corporate accounts with predictable needs closely tied to their budget cycles.

"Sell what you have" was the phrase that Dell developed for the crucial function of matching incoming demand to predetermined supply." – Islands of Profit in a Sea of Red Ink.

A review of Dell's process by Dr. Jonathan Byrnes reveals that Dell had a true S&OP process where the *"they revised the company's sales targets and production plan to reflect Dell's evolving situation"* and the *"sales commission plan was set to equal the production plan."*

The effect of all of this was to enable Sales and Supply Chain to actually play for the same team, unlike in most companies where Sales and Supply Chain fight against one another. In this way, Sales begins to **take responsibility for the service level** in a much more proactive way than simply setting service level goals that cannot be reached without fudging the service level measurement statistics. This is covered in detail in the SCM Focus Press book *Safety Stock and Service Levels: A New Approach.*

4. *The Difference Between the TPS and Associated Lean Initiatives*: As you will see from this list, many techniques that were applied by Toyota were never adopted when TPS/JIT/Lean were adopted for external consumption. Therefore, TPS/JIT/Lean presented to audiences outside of Japan is some type of Frankenstein monster that is more about marketing consulting services than about faithfully communicating what worked in these earlier incarnations.

Secondly, some techniques that are associated with TPS/JIT/Lean were never implemented by Toyota. One of these is ISO 9000, as the following quotation from *Factory Physics* indicates: *"Interestingly, Toyota tried ISO 9000 in one of its factories and then ceased using it because it added no value."*

In fact, according to *Factory Physics*, Toyota would have opposed the use of such certificates. *"To do so would indicate the reaching of some arbitrary target – the antithesis of continual improvement."*

5. *Diminution of the Importance of Collaboration*: Collaboration with supply chain partners was a big part of what made TPS successful. If a supplier was having problems meeting Toyota's quality or delivery schedule, a Toyota representative was sent to help the supplier. This intensive supply chain consulting was a critical part of how Toyota did business from the beginning.

However, Japan is a collectivist culture. The US and Europe are not. In the US, relationships with suppliers are often quite confrontational, with the larger entity, or the entity with the leverage, using the leverage as a hammer to get as many concessions as possible.[5]

---

[5] Walmart is tougher than most companies, but they treat their suppliers as completely subordinate entities. Suppliers to Walmart must meet Walmart's extremely demanding standards or be fined or otherwise punished. In fact, while companies are very focused on keeping their inventories lean, another major impact of what is often the abuse of power on the part of buyers with their suppliers is essentially making the supplier carry their inventory. This is not actually Lean because often the same inventory level is carried; what changes is who carries the inventory. That is, while the ordering lot sizes are reduced, the absolute level of inventory in the system has not. Inventory shifting of this nature, often justified on the basis of Lean principles, is now common in buyer-supplier relationships.

In fact, the collaborative aspects of the TPS have been diminished in importance by Lean proponents because they don't "sell" very well to US audiences. If you propose that one should really **be concerned about** the welfare of one's suppliers and should genuinely help them, the interpretation is that the individual making the statement is "soft." Therefore, the collaborative underpinning of the TPS has been diminished in order to improve the marketability of the concept of Western tastes.[6]

6. *The Diminution of the Importance of Unions*: Lean requires highly involved workers – those that have genuine autonomy. Toyota was unionized; something that tends to help get buy-in and input as unionized employees are better paid and have more rights than non-union employees.

In fact, Toyota's management studied Ford when developing TPS and came up with the following rather unflattering conclusion.

> *"The Toyota people also recognized that the Ford system had contradictions and shortcomings, particularly with respect to employees. With General Douglas MacArthur actively promoting labor unions in the occupation years, Ford's harsh attitudes and demeaning job structures were unworkable in post-war Japan. They were also unworkable in the American context, but that would not be evident for some years. America's 'Greatest Generation' carried over attitudes from the Great Depression that made the system work in spite of its defects.*
>
> *"Toyota soon discovered that factory workers had far more to contribute than just muscle power. This discovery probably originated in the Quality Circle movement. Ishikawa, Deming, and Juran all made major contributions to the quality movement. It culminated in team development and cellular manufacturing"*
> – A Brief History of Just in Time.

---

[6] Someone might reasonably debate how much of the relationship between Toyota and its suppliers was purely collaborative as Toyota had a great deal of leverage over suppliers as a) Toyota was a large portion of the supplier's business and b) Toyota executives often were on the boards of directors of their suppliers. This is part of the interlocking directorates that made up the Japanese system.

However, US consultants knew that US executives disliked unions and therefore, when TPS/JIT/Lean made the transition to the US in the form of books and consulting, the union side of the equation was left out of the process. US companies wanted all of the benefits of bought in employees, but without the employees actually being bought in.

Since the early 1970's, US companies have done their best to eliminate unions from the landscape and to distort the history of unions, painting them in the most pejorative way possible, and why not, unions fight for higher wages for employees, which reduces profits. This censoring of the TPS/JIT/Lean into what was most marketable meant that the TPS/JIT/Lean approaches that migrated from Japan to the US and to Europe were poor facsimiles of the real thing.

This is explained in the following quotation. *"They brought back, mostly, the superficial aspects like KANBAN cards and quality circles. Most early attempts to emulate Toyota failed because they were not integrated into a complete system and because few understood the underlying principles."* – A Brief History of Just in Time.

7. *Developed Under Post War Austerity:* Toyota, and other Japanese companies, developed techniques for dealing with the difficult economic circumstances following WWII. While the US was untouched after WWII, Japan had been heavily bombed. Clearly, setting up the supply chain for long production runs and large lot sizes was not going to be an effective strategy as the level of demand was very low.

Therefore, the TPS was developed under conditions of austerity. Under conditions of high and stable demand, using relatively small lot sizes is inefficient. However, under conditions of low and unstable demand, having long production runs and relatively large lot sizes leads to waste. This is not to say that the TPS was not continued as Japan's economy greatly improved and sales volumes greatly increased - it did.

The following quotation is from Taiichi Ohno, the main intellectual force behind the TPS: *"For decades America cut costs by mass producing fewer types of cars. It was an American work style – but not a Japanese one. Our problem was how to cut costs while producing a small number of many types of cars."*

But even Taiichi Ohno implies that often this approach was not followed in Japan, once production volumes increased: *"Then during the 15 year period beginning in 1959-1960, Japan experienced unusually rapid economic growth. As a result, mass production, American-style was still used effectively in many areas."* However, authors on TPS/Lean/JIT will often leave out the fact that these approaches were developed under a period of austerity.

8. *Overgeneralization of Applicable Manufacturing Types and Environments for TPS/Lean/JIT:* The manufacturing type is controlled by what product is made. Products that can be disassembled into their associated parts are called discrete manufactured products. Products that cannot are called process-manufactured products. A discrete product, which is produced in a near-continuous fashion, is referred to as repetitive manufactured.

   The manufacturing environment is determined by the replenishment trigger setting; so products that are replenished upon receipt of a sales order are make-to-order. Those that are replenished on the basis of a forecast are called make-to-stock. Toyota produced automobiles, which is a discrete manufacturing type and a make-to-stock (primarily, although cars can be ordered) manufacturing environment.

   Strategies that apply well to one manufacturing type and manufacturing environment often do not translate well to other environments. Performing a number of changeovers in the repetitive or high volume process industry manufacturing is simply not feasible.

   Therefore, simply because a strategy worked in one or several environments does not mean that it can be generalized to other environments. All that can be said when providing anecdotes of success is that the strategy might be effective in that environment, but other correlated factors must also be controlled, because the success that one company experiences is not necessarily entirely traceable to a single strategy. This leads to the next point.

9. *Misallocating the Reasons for the Japanese Manufacturing Success:* Many authors that write on TPS/Lean/JIT over-allocate the success of

Japanese companies to inventory management techniques. In the early stages of the Japanese export boom, roughly speaking the 1960's, Japan's currency was relatively weak - providing Japanese products with a cost advantage. From this time up until the 1980's, Japan became known for producing high quality and low cost products.

Even if Japanese companies had incurred more inventory costs by not following Lean production and inventory techniques, they would still have had a cost advantage in the export market due to the currency exchange rate. However, what really stood out with Japanese manufactured products was the quality level. This is a quality advantage that continues – although has narrowed – to this day.

If we look at automobiles, Japan's makes continue to be rated at a higher quality level than US, European, and Korean makes. In the 1970's, US car makers were producing low quality products that required frequent repair, as marketing for in all intents and purposes had effectively taken over US car manufacturers. Planned obsolescence, low quality, constant model changes, etc. ruled US car manufacturers. As a synopsis, the US car industry was an easy target for competitors that offered something better.

Consumers began noticing that Japanese cars did not need to be repeatedly serviced, and those with a focus on reliability tended to purchase Japanese cars. However, high quality is not correlated with low inventory levels, and is in fact **inversely** related to the production lot size. In fact, anyone who has actually worked on a manufacturing floor knows that quality **increases** with the volume produced. The more you do the same thing without changing, the higher the quality and the higher the output.

The lowest quality product is normally produced at the beginning of a production run. During this period the machines are tuned, tolerances are altered, and a higher percentage of the output product is not saleable. Longer production runs lead to higher quality and more uniform product.

To a person in manufacturing, the ultimate environment is one that never has the production line go down, except for scheduled maintenance.

And this is not some fantasy that I am describing. A blast furnace runs at constant temperature for years before being taken down for maintenance. Light bulbs and florescent tubes are produced in the repetitive manufacturing environment. These are high-speed dedicated lines that produce the same product in virtual perpetuity.

These environments have dedicated production lines – if you want to make another product, you simply have another production line. The speed of a dedicated repetitive manufacturing production line is something to behold up close, and the efficiency is awesome. Looms which produce textiles and petroleum refining operations are other examples of near-constant production runs that achieve amazing efficiency and output.

However, getting back to the point, **quality**, not Lean lot sizing approaches, was the primary reason for the rise of Japan as a manufacturing power.[7]

The subject of quality management is in fact another area of study from supply chain management or supply chain planning. As a person who configures supply chain systems, I can setup the system to operate in a Lean fashion, or oriented toward high efficiency, but this does not deter-

---

[7] If we turn to China, inventory management is also not at the root of China's rise as a manufacturing power and it is certainly not based upon quality, with the quality of manufactured products not only failing at much higher rates, but the products coming out of Chinese factories often not meeting the build specification. China leverages low wages, an artificially depressed currency, and extremely lax environmental regulations. Producing in China has actually reduced quality and safety (as unsafe chemicals are routinely found in Chinese products – however the reduced cost is simply so attractive that China developed seemingly overnight into a major manufacturing center).

Books generally don't focus on advantages based upon degrading the environment of a country, or on labor exploitation – because it does not fit with the positive, upbeat narrative that helps make writing digestible, providing the illusion that things are continually getting better.

That is, what is written is not necessarily what is true, but what is appealing to be read. However, there are multiple reasons for a country to rise in terms of manufacturing prominence, and these reasons change per country based upon the timeframe. For instance, the US was once a low cost manufacturing alternative to Britain.

mine the quality of the output product.[8] In fact, while longer production runs do provide quality advantages, I would never propose that anything I do in setting up a planning system has a relationship to the quality of the final output.

Different Types Manufacturing

In order to emphasize the variety of manufacturing types that exist, I have included a few of them from my book *Process Industry Manufacturing Software*.

---

[8] There are a number of Lean proponents that propose that JIT in particular is related to higher quality. The logic they propose is that inspection and quality assurance works better if work in process (or WIP) is low, and that JIT leads to low WIP environments. It seems this argument is greatly dependent upon the particular scenario, and again is over-applied.

First, even in a higher WIP environment, inspection can be performed before the WIP level grows. In fact, quality control and inspection should always happen throughout the operation (the operation being one processing step at one resource in the overall production run) regardless of whether a Lean or push production approach is being followed.

In fact, for decades, statistical process control has instilled the idea of quality checking not at the end of the operation, but continuously through the process. Obviously, it makes sense to prevent the production of out-of-specification material.

Secondly, it is hard to debate that JIT environments **do not** have a higher likelihood of starving machines and stopping the production run than an environment where the inventory levels are set in accordance with standard inventory management formulae, such as when MRP or another planning procedure is used.

If the production run is stopped because of inadequate inventory, the factory loses the quality benefit of the single, continuous production run. Therefore the argument in favor of JIT improving quality based upon quality inspection assumes an irresponsible and badly out of date assumption regarding how quality inspection is performed.

The lack of observation of the increased likelihood of shutting down an operation due to a WIP shortage, leading to operations runs, seems to indicate that the proposers of the relationship between JIT and supposed improvements in quality are not considering all of the factors of a real life manufacturing environment when they are making this particular proposal.

The Blast Furnace

Blast furnaces produce metals and are enormous. The technology goes back 2,000 years, although the technology was not distributed broadly until the thirteenth century.

This is a blast furnace. The giant pipe that connects to the top of the blast furnace carries coke, limestone flux, and iron ore to the top of the blast furnace where it is dropped into the furnace. The furnace itself is tall and cylindrical, with the bottom of the blast furnace being the hottest and the top being the coolest. Hot air is blasted into the side in order to maintain the combustion. Iron is removed from the bottom of the blast furnace.

The blast furnace maintains the highest efficiency when it is run continuously and, because it does just one thing, there is little need to turn it on or off. In fact, according to the Steelworks website, the blast furnace is typically run continuously for between four and ten years.

Textiles

One often thinks of textiles as simply the assembly of textiles into clothing, automotive seat covers, etc. These processes are labor intensive. However, the step prior to cutting and assembly is the actual creation of the textile material, and this step is in fact quite automated.

This is a massive loom that runs in a continuous fashion. Modern looms are connected to enormous banks of spindles, which serve as a near-constant supply of input material as the bank of spindles show on the following page.

Continuous processes require continual supplies of raw materials. Any shortage of raw materials would mean stopping the process, which would result in significant inefficiencies. Continuous manufacturing processes have the highest efficiency and the lowest per unit cost, but also the highest investments in machinery. Continuous manufacturing is the eventual state when variability has been controlled in the manufacturing process and the process has been fully automated. These looms are scaled up and more sophisticated versions of the following loom.

This loom can produce in small batches, in fact batches of one, or lot sizes. Each time the weaver produces a new blanket, they can get different colored yarn and a new template. There is a changeover cost; however, because of the low production rate and low efficiency, the changeover cost is not high. This is how manufacturing was performed prior to the Industrial Revolution. It is Lean, and it is customizable, but the output is low.

Weaving was once a manual activity, and in some parts of the world, it is still done that way. The first powered loom was invented in 1830 in England. Looms have become faster and more efficient ever since, to the point of sophistication where they are continuous operations.

A major part of our standard of living is based upon the increased productivity due to the scaling up and electrification of factories. This productivity increase was greater than all other productivity increases before and since - including the electronics and computing revolutions. This is why productivity gains spike so dramatically after 1820 - which saw the start of the period of the first industrial revolution. Right now, while you are reading this, giant looms are running 24/7, rotating at 1,200 RPM, turning out prodigious quantities of textiles at a very low cost. It's hard to appreciate the high speed and continuous nature of these looms until you see one in action. I have included a YouTube link that shows exactly this.

http://www.youtube.com/watch?v=V5e1YKkZFhc

This video shows the complexity that is involved in the set-up of this machine. Knowing this complexity, it would be hard to make the case that setting up all of the spindles to produce a different product would be a good use of time or the machine. This is a textbook example of continuous manufacturing processes: the efficiency of continual use is simply so high that it trumps many other factors.

The Lean Focus of This Book

Lean is partially a series of techniques for reducing waste, but is also a management approach. This is explained by the following quotation from *Factory Physics*:

> *"In setups and many other areas, the Japanese have taken a holistic, systems view of manufacturing of how these systems behave. Consequently, they have been able to identify policies that cut across traditional functions and to manage the interfaces between these functions. Thus while the specific techniques of JIT are important, the systems approach to transforming the manufacturing environment and the constant attention to detail over an extended period of time are fundamental."*

It involves things like coaching or mentorship. It would be illogical to compare the management approach that is Lean to the techniques of supply chain planning like supply and production planning procedures. Therefore, I am not going to attempt to do that.

Instead I will be taking an approach to Lean that focuses on its techniques, and specifically its techniques that are relevant to inventory. However, I do explain how one cannot take a reductionist view of the techniques employed by Lean proponents to explain the success of some of the companies that have employed Lean principles.

Conclusion

The origin of Lean is the Toyota Production System or TPS. However, the TPS drew parts of its approach from Ford Motor Company. I believe Lean is such a strong trend, in fact a trend that extends far beyond manufacturing, in large part because of dissatisfaction in the quality of the output from supply planning systems.

This dissatisfaction can stem anywhere from MRP's logic being overly simplistic to where implementing companies have run into problems implementing supply planning methods more complex than MRP/DRP. Lean holds that variability is the main problem in supply chains, and that management of variability should be a **main focus** of supply chain planning. This can entail either reducing the variability or placing buffers closest to the point of variability. (Reducing variability may be switching to a more reliable transportation company that delivers consistently.)

Interestingly, when I compared my research into Lean with how Lean is normally presented, I found the normal presentation to leave out important aspects of Lean and to be oversimplified to the degree that it loses much of its effectiveness. There is the authentic Lean and then the diluted Lean, which is designed to sell books and consulting services and to require that the audience never have many broadly accepted assumptions challenged.

Furthermore, Lean is neither the best strategy for every environment, nor for every part of the product location database. For example, product locations with high volume will not benefit from Lean.

CHAPTER 6

Where Lean and Reorder Points are Applicable

When to Use Reorder Point Planning

Items placed on a reorder point methodology could be placed there for the following reasons.

- *Forecastability*: They are difficult or impossible to forecast... or they have a level forecast because their demand history is so stable.

- *Lead Times*: Their supply is relatively unconstrained and their lead times are short.

Any products in these categories are essentially either not worth the effort to plan with more advanced methods, or advanced methods **do not add value to their planning over the simpler method of reorder point planning**. This does not seem to be a very well understood point by those that work in MRP/procedural planning. As is pointed out by E. A. Silver in his well-regarded paper on ideas related to inventory control for items with erratic demand patterns:

Most useable inventory control procedures are based upon assumptions about the demand distribution (e.g., unit sized transactions or normally distributed demand in a replenishment lead-time) that are invalid in the case of an erratic item. If this is not the case, the procedures tend to be computationally intractable.

This paper was written back in 1970. However, an enormous increase in computational power since that time has not made the problem **more "tractable."** Although often overlooked, all supply planning methods are designed to be used with products that can be forecasted within a certain accuracy range.

If the forecast accuracy is too low, the procedural methods of supply and production planning is undermined. If the forecast accuracy is extremely high, then reorder point planning can provide results of equal quality, but with much less effort. Procedural planning is the best fit for product location combinations with accuracy levels that are **neither too low nor too high**. Paradoxically, the understanding of where value can be added by supply planning procedures is different than this, with the concept being that the worse the forecast accuracy, the more a sophisticated planning system can add value.

There is a strong orientation within companies to create forecasts for all items in the product database. However, this does not necessarily mean that the forecast should actually be used for every product location combination in the supply planning system where a forecast is created in the demand planning system. However, for most companies at least, some portion of the product database cannot be reliably forecasted. Thus, forecasts are emphasized by demand planning for some product location combinations that add no value to the supply planning process.

Specifically, not all product location combinations can have their forecast improved by a more complex forecasting method (which is the continual hope of many) than a simple long-horizon moving average resulting in a **level** forecast. This applies equally to very stable products, as they also will use a **level** forecast. Reorder point planning for the finished good (as the associated finished and raw material supply plan is driven from the finished good supply plan) is an effective and low effort/low cost approach for product location combinations that fall into this category.

Reorder Point Planning for Deployment/Outbound Supply Planning

Up until this point, we have discussed reorder point planning for the initial supply plan, which generates the purchase requisitions and the planned production orders. However, replenishment/reorder parameters are available at all the locations in a supply network. Therefore, there is nothing to say that reorder point planning cannot be used throughout the entire supply network, both inbound to the plant or regional distribution center and outbound for deployment.

In this way, reorder point planning can be used for deployment, which would simply mean removing them from the product location combinations from the planning procedure that is used. With most supply planning applications that I have used, this is simple to do.

The business should be given the task of re-determining the reorder point parameters for the product locations that are to be transitioned off the active planning track. If they are new to doing this, they may need some outside help from someone with a strong mathematical understanding of how to create intelligent reorder points.

Conclusion

Reorder point planning is an early approach to supply chain planning; however, while often dismissed as passé, it actually has applicability in a number of circumstances. Reorder point planning can be used effectively for products that are **both easy and difficult** to forecast. What works well for products with erratic demand history works equally well for products with extremely stable demand history.

It is a relatively simple matter in a supply planning system to convert some product location combinations to pure reorder point planning and other product location combinations to being processed with a supply planning method. Furthermore, a product may be planned in one way at one location and **planned a second way** at a different location.

In fact, customizing the supply planning approach per the demand history at a product location rather than applying a blanket approach to all products will produce superior results. This is the primary topic of the SCM Focus Press book *Multi Method Supply Planning in SAP APO*.

CHAPTER 7

Determining When to use Lean verus MRP

Differentiating Planning From Physical Shop Floor Movements

Lean is really a combination of techniques that are based around principles that have already been covered up to this point. If we put aside the management and the process aspects of Lean for a moment, in terms of the specific techniques, some of them relate to planning, and are therefore competitive with MRP and other planning procedures, and others are related to execution movements that occur after planning is performed.

KANBAN (also developed by Taiichi Ohno) is a perfect example of one of these Lean techniques. KANBAN, as pointed out by Wikipedia, **is not** an inventory control system. Instead, KANBAN is a technique for scheduling the movement of material within a factory floor. KANBAN and other Lean techniques are very focused on keeping WIP as low as possible.

MRP, if capacity leveling is not performed, is only concerned with meeting demand. If capacity leveling is performed, then it is also concerned with scheduling production in a way that meshes with the capacity of the resources. Other planning methods, such as cost optimization, may be more sophisticated in terms of planning while accounting for constraints, but they are also unconcerned or are not designed to minimize WIP.[1]

The question becomes how to integrate two control mechanisms (MRP/planning and Lean/execution) in a way that leverages the best of each. While reorder points can be used, in most cases it is not desirable to use reorder points exclusively for planning.

On the other hand, MRP/planning does not have much to "say" with respect to what happens after the plan is generated. Certainly, any planning method can be rerun up until the product is produced; however while many companies do this, it does not make very much sense to.

MRP and similar planning systems have a frozen period which declares a timeline where changes are not to be made. This frozen period in the supply and production planning system determines the hand-off of responsibility for managing the activity. If a company has a one-week frozen period, then changes should not be made, and in fact MRP should not even be run for this period.

---

[1] In fact, it would not be difficult at all to add the functionality to planning systems that would place a restriction on the size of WIP, although it would be a serious maintenance issue as the WIP would most likely have to be set at some percentage of the production order.

A capacity-leveled planning system like MRP, or a constraint-based system, would then stop loading the production line when either the bottleneck resource was overloaded or the WIP "cap" was met. More likely, only one WIP cap would need to be set per production line as the various WIP locations along the production line are, of course, directly related.

Therefore, a cap on one WIP location would effectively cap them all. In this case, the WIP location that was capped would naturally be called the bottleneck WIP. The WIP cap would need to be not simply focused on minimizing WIP because it is very important in allowing the efficient utilization of machines that have different production rates.

Some machines simply perform a much more complex process than other machines. WIP allows the creation of a buffer between a low throughput workstation and a high throughput workstation so that there is minimal machine downtime. Therefore WIP must be set to serve a number of objectives. According to the book *Factory Physics*, if a WIP cap is used, then the system may be considered "pull."

This can be easily controlled in the system in its configuration. Continuing to run MRP for this period produces two undesirable outcomes. First, it of course moves the schedule around – but secondly, it creates confusion as to what mechanism is in control of the process. Frozen periods are very appropriate because the frozen period in the MRP system declares when MRP **no longer controls what is happening** and the responsibility for the production and procurement shifts to another system, and often another group of people.

MRP and Forecastability

MRP and all other supply planning procedures are forecast-based planning methods. They all assume a certain level of forecast accuracy, which in turn assumes a certain level of forecastability on the part of the product location combinations. However, if we consider the environment where Lean was developed in Japan, we can see that Toyota was facing a situation of low forecastability:

> *"Levels of demand in the Post War economy of Japan were low and the focus of mass production on lowest cost per item via economies of scale therefore had little application. Having visited and seen supermarkets in the USA, Taiichi Ohno recognized the scheduling of work should not be driven by sales or production targets but by actual sales. Given the financial situation during this period, over-production had to be avoided, and thus the notion of Pull (build to order rather than target driven Push) came to underpin production scheduling."*
>
> - Wikipedia

Many products that are difficult to forecast have no discernible pattern in their demand history, and no mathematical algorithm can create a good forecast without one. This is a well-observed phenomenon, is increasing as a trend, and is in great part driven by forces inside, rather than outside, of the company.

> *"Nearly every company is 30 t0 40 percent unprofitable by any measure. In almost every company, 20 to 30 percent of the business is highly profitable, and a large proportion of this profitability is going to cross-subsidize the unprofitable part of the business. The rest of the company is marginal. The most current metrics and control systems*

(budgets, etc.) do not even show the problem or the opportunity for improvement."

- Islands of Profit in a Sea of Red Ink

"Some managers argue that it is a good idea to accept business that contributes, even marginally, to covering overhead. However, when you take on a lot of business that contributes only marginally to overhead, in almost all cases it will absorb a significant amount of sales and operations resources that otherwise would have been devoted to increasing your "good" business. And it will remain and grow into the embedded profitability that drags down earnings in company after company.

"If the underlying reason for taking marginal business is to fill unused capacity, you need a sunset policy to stop taking the marginal business once capacity is filled and to remove it when full freight business is available. Not many companies have the information and discipline to do this."

– Islands of Profit in a Sea of Red Ink

So first, most companies carry far too many products, which reduces forecast-ability. This is referred to as product proliferation.

Product Proliferation
Product proliferation is the increase in the number of products that are carried. Often the marketing differences between the products are only incidental and illusory. Proliferation would be even worse than it currently is, but retailers only have so much space to offer. An excellent example of product proliferation is toothpaste.

Most of these toothpaste containers essentially contain a similar set of chemical compounds; however, marketing provides customers with different varieties of what is often the same product in order to promote purchases. Many of the claims are unfounded, but because there is very little regulation (in the US at least), they can say what they like regarding what the toothpaste will do for consumers.

Whether something is true or not is barely mentioned (that is what is written on the packaging), and anyone who might bring this up is considered hopelessly naïve, as the primary focus is whether or not the claim will increase sales.

This is the problem – when you create incentives for groups that are entirely focused on maximizing sales, it is quite predictable that the company will metastasize into areas that are not profitable.

There may be no better example of an industry that has gone to the extreme with unnecessary product proliferation as the grocery industry. The typical US grocery store has between 35,000 and 50,000 SKU's, which is a massive increase in SKU's over the past several decades. When standing, one can no longer see over most grocery store shelves. However, one grocery chain takes a different path, and this is a major reason they perform so much better than the industry average. I covered Trader Joe's in my first forecasting book, *Supply Chain Forecasting Software*.

A basic principle of Lean is smooth production. This is referred to as Heijunka and the approach to smoothing production through scheduling is called the Heijunka Box. In fact, one of the "Seven Zeros" described by Edward Deming and which outlines the ideal production environment is Zero Surging.

However, Sales and Marketing are destroying the Heijunka! This is because of their insistence in having the company carry so many products and having them available at such high service levels. Toyota controlled its demand variability by controlling the product mix. This is explained in the following quotation from *Factory Physics*:

> *"Toyota's product design and marketing were so successful that demand for its cars consistently exceeded supply. This helped in several ways. First, Toyota was able to limit the number of options of cars produced. A maroon Toyota would always have maroon interior. Second, Toyota could establish a production schedule months in advance. This virtually eliminated all demand variability seen by the manufacturing facility."*

Thus Toyota controlled most of the demand variability, which left it only with manufacturing and supplier variability. Therefore, Lean and the high variability of demand that is self-generated within companies by Sales and Marketing is a poor fit for Lean – something I have never heard brought up. Of course, product proliferation is only one of the negative externalities caused by Sales and Marketing - another is promotions.

Promotions

In many companies, Sales and Marketing increasingly view promotions as a major part of the overall strategy. Promotions have greatly increased in their frequency and, according to Gartner, roughly 20 percent of the revenue of manufacturers is spent on promotions, up from 0.5 percent in 1985.[2] This is one of the largest increases of **any expense item**.

---

[2] Hagemeyer,Dale. *Vendor Panorama for Trade Promotion Management in Consumer Goods*. Gartner, 2012.

For many consumer packaged goods companies, promotions are the majority of their overall advertising expense.[3] Furthermore, the use of promotions is likely to increase in the future, as one of the limitations to performing more promotions is related to technology - something that vendors of promotion management software are alleviating by increasing the sophistication of their software. We can tell because it's evident in the marketing literature of software vendors that sell promotion management software to companies. Retalix is one of the software vendors that specializes in this type of software.

> *"With hundreds of promotions happening across thousands of items
> simultaneously, oftentimes more than one department is promoting
> the same item,' said Bob Smith, product manager for Retalix Loyalty.
> 'This becomes a critical business problem for everyone involved,
> because not only will the item have a lower margin, it can even sell at
> a loss.'"*

In fact, software vendors ranging from JDA to IBM to Junction Solutions make promotion management software, and this category of software is quite broadly implemented at CPG clients. All of these applications are singularly focused on allowing companies to implement increased numbers of, and increased complexity of, promotions. However, these applications do nothing to update the promotion information in the forecasting system.

Of course, any system can have its data extracted and put into another system with an interface, but this is clearly not the focus of the marketing literature of these software vendors. They also do not bother to mention the fact that there is increased overhead in accounting for promotions in demand history. They are simply focused on selling their software to companies by offering them tantalizing options to run increasingly complex promotions. Once again, the line of reasoning is that promotions are "free." They are actually "all benefit and no cost."

What is at least somewhat amusing is that JDA, which sells this promotion management software, also sells forecasting software. However, once again,

---

[3] Lucas, Anthony. "In-Store Trade Promotions – Profit or Loss?" *Journal of Consumer Marketing*. April 1, 1996.

JDA's marketing literature on promotion management software makes **no mention** of the overhead and complexity that all of these complicated promotions create for forecasting generally.

Therefore, just as with the corporate buyers of software that often work towards conflicting objectives, JDA as a software vendor does the same thing in its software lines. It offers functionality to Sales and Marketing that optimizes their needs at the expense of forecasting, while offering a forecasting solution that then attempts to deal with the extra forecasting complexity driven by the promotions that the company can now run more of because they purchased JDA's promotion management software. All of this is covered in detail in the SCM Focus Press book *Promotions Forecasting: Techniques of Forecast Adjustments in Software*.

Sales and Marketing still feels quite hamstrung by not being able to run more promotions. Some in Sales and Marketing question whether there may be too many promotions and whether they have negative consequences, but most of the sentiment lies with increasing the use of promotions.

> *"CPG companies often spend anywhere from 8 percent to 20 percent of revenue on promotions. Various studies suggest that anywhere from 25 to 70 percent of CPG suppliers' trade promotion spend (their expenditure) is ineffective. Some quick math suggests that for every billion dollars in revenue, at least $20 million to $50 million, and likely significantly more, is being poorly spent. That is a substantial amount of money that could be better applied to product innovation or other more significant drivers of growth and brand equity."*
> - Uncovering the Hidden Costs of Trade Promotions

Promotions are an added complexity to any business. There is what is referred to as a churn, which is caused by constant promotions, introducing chaos into the management of products. Lean proponents talk a great deal about reducing mura, which is Japanese for unevenness. However, promotions produce nothing but unevenness.

Lean uses a variety of techniques for keeping mura in check such as control charts which leverage statistical process control. However that can only help control for unevenness that is part of the supply chain process – but promotions are unevenness that is imposed from **outside** the supply chain process. The entire concept of the control chart is that the root cause of the variability is found and then addressed.

However, the root cause of promotion variability cannot be addressed because, at the majority of US and European companies, supply chain does not have any influence over the number of promotions run by Sales and Marketing.[4] No control chart will help with this type of unevenness because it requires confrontation with the Sales and Marketing entities that are responsible for the unevenness.

> *"We have found that trade promotions can play havoc with the*
> *sales forecasting process, creating promotion-driven seasonality in*
> *historical sales data when distributors increase their inventories in*
> *response to periodic price promotions from manufacturers rather*
> *than to anticipated increases in consumer demand."*
> – Sales Forecasting Management

If you read a typical book or article that covers this topic, there is often a great willingness to point out that the product database has "exploded" and that product life cycles are decreasing, but a great unwillingness to explain why this is the case. The reader is left with the definite impression that all of these changes are driven by the market, when in actual fact, companies themselves, and more specifically Sales and Marketing within these companies, are driving these changes. I believe that it is misleading the reader to not point out that much of these changes are in fact self-imposed by the company itself.

Determining Forecastability
Products that have a very stable history exist at the other end of the continuum of forecast difficulty. Typically, it is very easy to forecast for products with a stable demand history; however, if this is the case, actively forecasting the product does not add very much value to supply planning (the ultimate consumer of the demand plan) because a product with stable demand history

---

[4] I can't speak to the influence over promotions that supply chain might have in other
   regions outside of the US and Europe.

does not need to be forecasted. Products with stable demand can be managed effectively and efficiently with reorder point logic, where orders are based upon a reorder point or a reorder period.

Intermittent - or "lumpy" - demand is one of the most common features of a product's demand history that makes a product unforecastable. Service parts are the best-known example of a product with lumpy demand. However, I have come across intermittent demand in many different types of companies. For instance, one of my clients was a textbook publisher. A large percentage of their product database had an intermittent demand history, which would normally not be expected of this type of product.

However, due to the fact that different US states buy textbooks in large volumes whenever funding comes through, the demand ends up being quite unpredictable for many books. A school system will not make any purchase for some time and then will buy many textbooks all at once. For example, California is on a seven-year procurement cycle, which means they wait seven years between purchases.

Examples of Unforecastable Demand

The central premise of this chapter is that many products are inherently unforecastable. As was stated earlier, a lack of forecastability can be determined mathematically and it can also be determined visually. I find that displaying the graphics of unforecastable products is an educational exercise, and I have used this technique with clients to get the point across. A visual representation of unforecastability is better, in my view, than representing the same thing with a series of numbers in columns.

The following graphics are examples of unforecastable demand history. An analysis of each is provided below the screen shot:

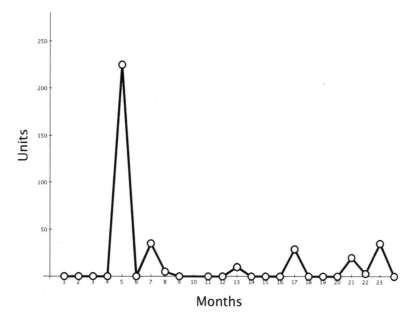

This product is clearly statistically unforecastable as there is no discernible pattern. This product has one demand peak in month seven (July), and several other smaller demand points, but simply not enough to forecast another demand point. This is a fairly obvious unforecastable demand pattern. The next example is a bit more complicated.

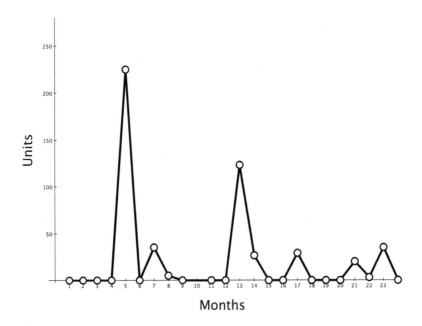

In this case, there are two demand peaks, and it might appear to be a good bet that the demand peak will repeat a third time...except it is not a good bet, because the first peak is in month five (May) of the first year, and the second peak is in month one, (January) in the second year. Where this product is going next is anyone's guess. This product is also unforecastable.

Managing Products With No Forecast With Supply Planning

When speaking of supporting supply planning, it is in fact not necessary to forecast the entire product database. However, the vast majority of companies think that they should and they do so. The only products that can be forecasted using statistical forecasting are those that have a discernible pattern of demand, and not all products have this. Without a discernable pattern, no mathematical forecasting method can beat a many-period moving average.

In many cases, the most effective approach of dealing with products that are very hard to forecast (or so easy to forecast that forecasting becomes unnecessary) is to simply remove their forecast from the supply planning process – although they will typically still be forecasted by the demand planning systems – and these forecasts can be used for other purposes.

These product location combinations can be placed on reorder point planning. At one company I consulted for, reorder point planning could have been used for around **half** of the product database. The percentage varies by the product type and the activities of the company, among other variables.

Reorder point planning works for both items with uniform consumption and erratic consumption. In the case of difficult to forecast items, they have an erratic demand history. The reorder quantity is therefore high and the safety stock is high. Because it cannot be predicted when demand will arrive, there is no other solution than to carry a large amount of stock (relative to average monthly demand) in order to be able to fulfill demand when it arrives.

This is simple to do with reorder point planning. For stable items, the amount of stock (average monthly demand) is low. Safety stock is relatively low. Therefore, reorder points actually work for both types of demand history; however the distinction is how high, relative to average demand, the stocking level can be set, as well as the reorder quantity (or reorder duration).

> *"The reorder point, on the other hand, always orders materials whenever the on-hand balance is below the reorder point, regardless of whether more is actually needed. In this case, there is enough on hand to satisfy the demands. But the reorder point system doesn't look at what is needed. Instead, it blindly attempts to keep a certain amount of inventory on hand at all times.*

> *"Examples show that reorder points are an obsolete technique - an invalid inventory model - and should not be used in any situations where inventory is maintained. They simply do not provide the visibility to see when product is actually needed and when problems are likely to occur." - Distribution Requirements Planning*

This criticism of reorder point planning only **holds for forecastable items**. However, for erratic demand items, the system cannot "look at what is needed" because it is inherently unknowable. The fact that the item has such a high forecast error means that the supply planning system is already "blind."

Applying a supply planning method does not change this fact. For highly stable products, the reorder point that is set can easily order the right amount. Items with a stable demand pattern are easy to model with reorder points, so it is in fact not blind at all. There is simply little benefit to passing a forecast to the supply planning system in this scenario.

> *"It is normally reserved for products without dependent requirements, like spare parts or consumables. However, it is also possible to use reorder point planning in combination with future requirements. An example of use for products with an erratic demand, like spare parts for customer service."*   – Delaware Consulting

This is not necessarily a criticism of reorder point planning; however, I do not see how reorder point planning should be limited to products without dependent requirements. Reorder points can be set in the supply planning system for finished goods, and then the BOM can be exploded with or without MRP for all the dependent items. I do, however, agree that it makes little sense to set dependent products on reorder point planning.

> *"Manual reorder points are even less effective in larger organizations. When an organization must plan across a large enterprise, particularly a vertically integrated enterprise, it is left with few viable and satisfactory options.*
>
> *The lack of visibility means that organizations of size or even moderate complexity are flying blind to the overall materials and inventory picture. Furthermore, manual reorder points and KANBANs do not consider the bill of materials in its totality. The KANBAN is defined only at each discrete connection. This means that stock positions must be placed at every position in the bill of material. This strategy, in turn, increases the number of stocked positions to manage and potentially raises total inventory."*
>   – Orlicky's Material Requirements Planning (3rd Edition)

Orlicky criticizes reorder point planning from several directions in this quotation. The clearest way to address each of his points is to list them one by one in a numbered format.

1. The size of the enterprise is irrelevant to whether reorder point planning should be used and, in fact, Orlicky provides no evidence to support the statement as to "why" this would be organization-size dependent. Rather than the organization, instead it is the attributes of the product demand history that determine whether reorder point planning should be used.

2. The statement regarding a lack of visibility is, again, true for erratic demand products no matter what method is used. A poor forecast accuracy means that visibility is by definition lacking. Using a supply planning method does not change the basic unforecastability of a product. "Visibility" is, in fact, provided by simply setting the reorder point to something that is consistent with the average demand.

3. Reorder points do not have to consider bill of materials in their totality because, as I stated earlier, they can only be set for the finished good. All dependent demand can be extrapolated from a BOM explosion without MRP, or a BOM explosion with MRP.

   Something that needs to be considered by critics of reorder point planning, but seems to be frequently ignored, is that it is unnecessary for all items in the BOM to be planned the same way.

All of the criticisms listed above, as well as the criticisms generally, suffer from a need to make a universal statement regarding the usability of reorder point planning when a universal statement cannot be made. Reorder point planning is useful under certain conditions.

One might think that it's not really possible to simply stop using the forecast generated by the demand planning system for supply planning. In fact, it is quite possible and easy to implement, although there can be a fair amount of complexity in the methods designed to calculate reorder points (something that is not commonly understood by those that oppose reorder point planning on the grounds that it is too simple).

In the SCM Focus Press book *Supply Planning with MRP/DRP and APS Software*, I cover reorder point planning differently than it is covered in a number of supply planning books, so I won't repeat the information here. Suffice it to say that there are many cases where it is better not to send a forecast to the supply planning system, and the supply planning system will still manage quite well. Therefore, a simple moving average forecast can be sent for unforecastable products, or no forecast at all.

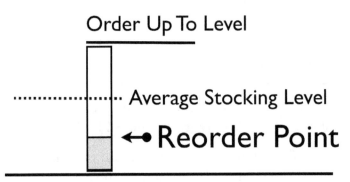

Reorder point setting does not require a forecast because the order is placed when the inventory drops to a certain level. However, there is not one "right way" of doing this. Regardless, the company gets away from continuing to invest effort in forecasting unforecastable products.

Analyzing the forecastability of the product database is one of the important steps to moving toward a more effective way of managing the forecasting process. For some products, a more advanced forecasting method cannot reasonably be expected to be an improvement over a simple, long duration, moving average forecast.

A number of trends are reducing forecastability of the product database, including actions by Marketing (such as promotions) and SKU proliferation (spreading the same demand over more products). Interestingly, the connection is not frequently made between these trends and forecastability. The more erratic demand becomes, the less forecasting can add value, and increased amounts of inventory must be carried to ensure that sufficient inventory exists when demand does arrive. This fact is lost on people who are unfamiliar with forecasting.

The Concept of Coding a Product Location Database

Companies tend to not properly code their product location database so that different product locations can be treated appropriately by the system. However, this coding can be valuable so that a short code can tell anyone who works with the product location combination (PLC) both the basic properties of the PLC, but also how the PLC is set up in system.

This coding is not static, because the PLC is periodically reviewed, or reviewed based upon market intelligence. However, if the coding is kept up to date, it can be very useful for a number of supply chain planning purposes.

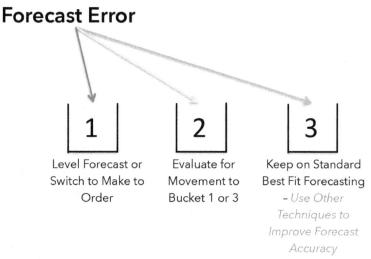

Master Data Review Cycle

As was explained earlier, the PLCs must be reviewed and updated on a periodic cycle. However, PLCs differ in terms of their review. Before computers were available, PLCs were placed on a review cycle for actually calculating order quantities. A review cycle might look something like this:

- Products 11234 to 11500 – 1st Monday of the Month

- Products 11500 to 15340 – 2nd Tuesday of the Month

- Products 15341 to 16201 – 3rd Wednesday of the Month

Computers did not compute the order quantities; this was something that had to be performed by inventory analysts. When computers did arrive on the scene, software vendors began touting their "perpetual inventory" abilities. This meant that when a goods receipt was recorded, the inventory was immediately recalculated. This also allowed companies to carry less inventory because, prior to computers, safety stock had to not only cover variability in lead time and forecasts, but also the longer period between reviews.

In a computerized system, if a larger than forecasted order comes in, it may reduce the planned stock below the reorder point - and the instantaneous calculation will cause a new order to be generated. In a manual periodic review system, that product may need to wait until recalculation by an inventory analyst (unless the analysts reviewed all of the large orders and then recalculated just those PLCs ahead of the rest of the PLCs in their rotation.) Interestingly, the book *Decision Systems for Inventory Management and Production Planning* does propose an advantage to periodic review and periodic ordering.

Items may be produced on the same piece of equipment, purchased from the same supplier, or shipped in the same transportation mode. In any of these situations, coordination of replenishment may be attractive. In such a case, periodic review is particularly appealing in that all items in a coordinated group can be given the same review interval. In contrast, under continuous review, a replenishment decision can be made at practically any moment in time; hence the load is less predictable. A rhythmic, rather than random, pattern is usually more appealing to the staff.

This master data review cycle concept is the same concept as was applied previously to inventory management, but of course a lot less work because this review cycle is for setting master data and prevents the settings from falling out of date. This is also important because master data is often changed in reaction to short-term needs, but then not changed back. This is an important quality checking process as well as an important process for adjusting the PLCs as things change over time.

Conclusion

Now that we have identified the PLCs that will go out on either the appropriate procedure or Lean approach, the next step is actually implementing this coding in a system. Of course, there are a wide number of systems out there that perform supply planning, so it is difficult to guess exactly the system that you, the reader, will be using. However, by providing an example it should be able to replicate the configuration in your supply planning system.

In ERP systems, there are really only two methods that can be used. There is MRP for the initial supply and production planning run, and then DRP for the deployment planning run. Reorder points can also be used at any product location combination. In APS systems, there are many more options for the supply planning method. However, each product location combination can be coded for any of these procedures, or for reorder point planning. How to implement this in systems will be the subject of the next chapter.

CHAPTER 8

Mixing Lean and Reorder Points with MRP-Type Planning

Much time is spent debating among the different supply planning methods, but far less is spent on how to properly integrate multiple methods into a cohesive strategy. That is unfortunate because all methods and method modifiers can be of value in some circumstances.

Arriving at the right combination of supply planning methods requires a detailed study of all the requirements and data necessary to drive the method. Without that upfront effort and knowledge, a method can end up being selected, and then simply be perpetuated because of the strong tendency not to change decisions after they have been made. In this chapter, I will use the example of SAP APO to illustrate how to configure the use of various methods. This is from a real project, and while the system that is used will change, the approach outlined in this chapter would apply to any supply planning application.

| Product Location Combination | | Advanced Methods | | Heuristic | | | | |
Product	Location	CTM	Optimizer	Heuristic With No Modifier	Reorder Point (Forward Calc)	Reorder Point (Non-Forward Calc) - Customized	Target Days Supply	Target Stock Levels
123	San Diego	X						
123	San Francisco				X			
123	Los Angeles			X				
123	San Jose					X		
567	San Diego	X						
657	San Francisco							X
Characteristics of Each Method								
Uses a Forecast?		Yes	Yes	Yes	No	Yes	Yes	No
Product is Forecastable?		Yes	Yes	Yes	No	Yes	Yes	No
Constrained Method?		Yes	Yes	No	No	No	No	No

Here is a screen shot taken from the SCM Focus Press book Multi Method Supply Planning in SAP APO. It shows the association of each product location combination with either the advanced method (either CTM – Capable to Match or the optimizer) or consumption-based replenishment methods.

In SAP APO, some methods need to work with what I refer to as method modifiers. In SAP APO, or more specifically SAP SNP (the supply planning module of APO), reorder point planning is a **modifier** of the heuristic method. The reorder point is just one of the modifiers that works with the SNP heuristic. Not all modifiers work with all of the methods. How this works is explained in the following graphic:

(Major) Planning Method	Reorder Point	Target Stock Level	Target Days Supply	Maximum Stock Level	Lot Size (Units)	Period Lot Size
Reorder Point, TSL, TDS, Max Stock Level, and Lot Size and Major Supply Planning Methods						
SNP Heuristic	X	X	X	X	X	X
Capable to Match						
SNP Optimizer				X	X	.

In the matrix above, the method is documented per product location. As you can see, the reorder point and the target stock level (TSL) only work with the SNP heuristic and are ignored by CTM and the optimizer. An important consideration for determining when to use one supply planning method over another is whether the product location combination is forecastable.

The above matrix can be used to help explain how to make selections between the various supply planning methods. Once this has been explained, the business subject matter experts can go off and code the entire product location database for each method that is used.

There is much more to a successful configuration than simply assigning product locations to profiles and then running the profiles. There is a sequence in which the profiles of the different methods must be run in order for the system to work properly. As such, testing must be performed to make the desired assignments between the supply planning method and the product location combination workable and to set up the profiles in the proper sequence. We will get into all of the detail on this topic in the following chapter.

Background on the Configuration of Multiple Supply Planning Methods

Once a company decides to use multiple supply planning methods, the next question is how to implement this in the system's configuration. How to do this is not widely understood or even explained. The SCM Focus Press book *Multi*

Method Supply Planning in SAP APO is one of the first to describe how to implement multiple supply planning methods in the configuration of any external supply chain planning system.

It would be most convenient if using multiple supply planning methods could simply be accomplished by assigning every product location a supply planning method and have the supply plan be created in a logical and consistent manner.

Unfortunately, making multiple methods work together is a good deal more complex than this because of how APO was developed. In this chapter, I will describe how combining multiple methods can be accomplished with the following methods and method modifiers:

1. Capable to Match (CTM)

2. The SNP Heuristic with:
    a. A Reorder Point
    b. A Target Stock Level
    c. A Target Days' Supply

The same principle and testing as discussed in this chapter applies to collaboratively using other supply planning methods; however, for any SNP heuristic method modifiers (reorder point, target stocking level, target days' supply), either of the other two modifiers (target stock level or target days' supply) could be set the same way as the reorder point I describe here. Within SNP, there are several ways of setting up a reorder point, target stock level, or target days' supply. For the purposes of this demonstration, I will show the most basic settings for each.

Here is a screenshot showing the reorder point as set in the product-location master:

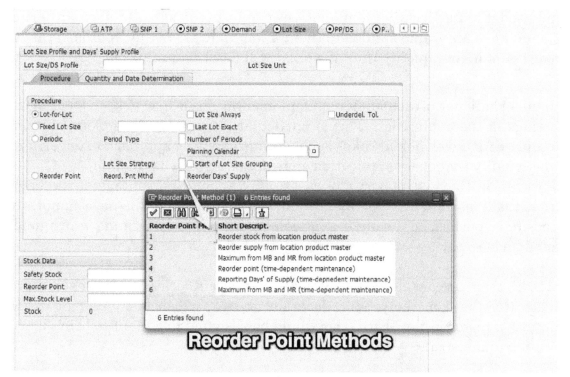

Reorder Point Methods

There are six different reorder point settings in SNP. However, for our purposes, there is no need to use anything but the simplest method. The time-dependent maintenance reorder points are used when the company has an interest in allowing planners to alter the reorder point per time.

On an actual project, it is important to provide all of the alternatives for each setting that are within the scope of the project.

When following a multi-method approach, it's important to have a good tool for assigning which method (and method modifier) is to be applied to which product location combination, as well as for keeping track of these assignments. Even though companies have a very large number of product location combinations, the assignment of methods and method modifiers does not have to be an onerous task.

First, a company already has method modifiers set up in their ERP system or external planning system (if they are migrating from another system such as Manugistics). These modifier values can be extracted from the existing system and used. Product location combinations can be grouped based upon any criteria and have any value applied to them. I am unaware of any approach that is faster or of higher quality than the one I will describe in this chapter.

A major challenge of all application implementations is how to keep track of the settings in the application. This is particularly true of SAP implementations because SAP development takes such a comprehensive approach to developing functionality that every application ends up with a very large number of fields. However, in the vast majority of cases, only a small percentage of the fields are actually used in an implementation. Therefore, one of the most important steps to be performed during the implementation is to determine which fields should have values assigned to them by the business.

In SNP, there are a wide variety of fields in different locations. However, many fields are stored in the product location master, which is equivalent to the material master in SAP ERP (this would be assigned to a plant to bring in the location dimension).

There are hundreds of fields in the product location master in SAP APO. Most companies only have the values in these fields managed in SAP or whatever system they use. However, that is not the best way to manage their fields. The parameters should be kept in an external database for the following reasons:

1. *Comparing and Contrasting:* Product location data cannot be easily compared and contrasted inside of the system, beyond bringing up the product location master for two combinations in different windows.

2. *Productivity:* Productivity is greatly enhanced when planners have access to the product location data in an easily accessible form.

3. *Visibility*: A common problem with product location data is enhanced with this approach, reducing the likelihood that this data will become out of date.

4. *Metadata:* A product location spreadsheet can include descriptions and comments in a way that SAP cannot. (Descriptions can be found by hitting F1 from any field. However, descriptions can be placed right into a spreadsheet, and can also be customized - and typically truncated to just the information that is of interest.)

My preferred way of storing this data is in a spreadsheet, which allows for the filtering of values, the use of Pivot Tables for analysis, and other advanced data capabilities in Excel. This approach applies to setting the overall policies during the initial implementation and to continued maintenance. Once changes have been made to the spreadsheet, they can be made in most systems with a mass maintenance transaction.

Product Location Master Coding Spreadsheet

Field	Product	Location	Planning Method	ATP: Checking Horizon in Days	ATP: Checking Horizon Calendar	Goods Receipt Processing Time
Description			The supply planning method for a product location combination	Defines a time interval (checking date + period) in which a product availability check can be carried out.	The calendar for the checking horizon is used to calculate the end of the checking horizon. It is calculated in work days.	The time between the delivery or the production of a product and its availability as stock.
	White Wine	San Diego Factory	CTM constrained	5	5	2
	White Wine	San Francisco RDC	CTM constrained	5	5	2
	White Wine	San Jose DC	CTM constrained	5	5	2
	White Wine	Encinitas Semi Finished Factory	CTM unconstrained	0	0	1
	White Wine	La Mesa Component Factory	Reorder stock (forward calc basis) from location product master (units)	0	0	1
	White Wine	Napa Semi Finished Factory	Reorder Target Days Supply from location product master (enter days)	0	0	1

This is just a sample of the fields in the product location spreadsheet, and is all that I could fit into this screenshot. There are, of course, many fields on the product location master. Not all of them are filled in, but it is beneficial to note all of them in the spreadsheet, along with their definitions, so that planners can chose which to enable.

While it can seem intimidating to fill in all the fields of a spreadsheet like this, in fact the fields are rarely filled in one-by-one. It is much more common to group the products for a specific field. Spreadsheets also allow for the applications of IF/THEN formulae, which can auto-populate some field values based upon the values of one or more other fields.

Steps to Creating the Product-Location Spreadsheet/Database

On the following page, I list the steps to creating this product location spreadsheet, as well as the uses of the product location spreadsheet.

Creation Steps and Uses of the Product-Location Spreadsheet		
Question	Answer Number	Answers
Usages of the Product-Location Spreadsheet	1	Use a master data mass update tool in order to make the product-location master match the settings in the product-location spreadsheet.
	2	Use the product-location spreadsheet as a reporting device (the spreadsheet can be filtered, sorted, and other Excel data management functions can be used to provide quick evaluation of the settings). Alternatively, the spreadsheet can be imported into a BI application for company-wide reporting.

Once created, the product location spreadsheet can be reused for many purposes. The following are uses of the product location spreadsheet:

Creation Steps and Uses of the Product-Location Spreadsheet		
Question	*Answer Number*	*Answers*
Creation Steps of the Product-Location Spreadsheet	1	From evaluating the design, select the fields from the product-location master which may be used by the company.
	2	Review the fields with the business subject matter experts.
	3	Have the business subject matter experts go through and "code" the product-location spreadsheet for every possible product-location combination.

This way of managing settings for applications is quite sustainable, provides a great deal of visibility into the settings and allows for analysts to easily compare and contrast the parameters.

There are some applications, such as BarloWorld's Optimiza application, that build similar functionality right into the user interface, but these types of applications are few and far between. Therefore, in most cases, companies implement software that does not offer this type of functionality. This approach to application settings is quite unusual, as can be seen in the screen shot of Barloworld on the following page:

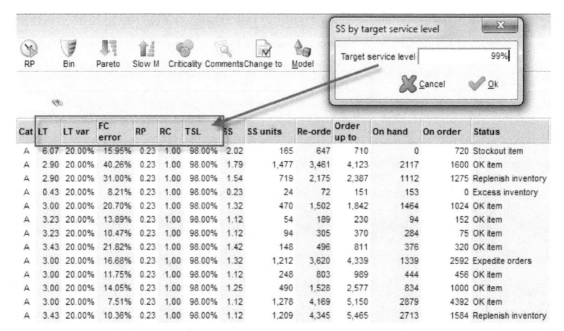

Cat	LT	LT var	FC error	RP	RC	TSL	SS	SS units	Re-orde	Order up to	On hand	On order	Status
A	6.07	20.00%	15.95%	0.23	1.00	98.00%	2.02	165	647	710	0	720	Stockout item
A	2.90	20.00%	40.26%	0.23	1.00	98.00%	1.79	1,477	3,461	4,123	2117	1600	OK item
A	2.90	20.00%	31.00%	0.23	1.00	98.00%	1.54	719	2,175	2,387	1112	1275	Replenish inventory
A	0.43	20.00%	8.21%	0.23	1.00	98.00%	0.23	24	72	151	153	0	Excess inventory
A	3.00	20.00%	20.70%	0.23	1.00	98.00%	1.32	470	1,502	1,842	1464	1024	OK item
A	3.23	20.00%	13.89%	0.23	1.00	98.00%	1.12	54	189	230	94	152	OK item
A	3.23	20.00%	10.47%	0.23	1.00	98.00%	1.12	94	305	370	284	75	OK item
A	3.43	20.00%	21.82%	0.23	1.00	98.00%	1.42	148	496	811	376	320	OK item
A	3.00	20.00%	16.68%	0.23	1.00	98.00%	1.32	1,212	3,620	4,339	1339	2592	Expedite orders
A	3.00	20.00%	11.75%	0.23	1.00	98.00%	1.12	248	803	989	444	456	OK item
A	3.00	20.00%	14.05%	0.23	1.00	98.00%	1.25	490	1,528	2,577	834	1000	OK item
A	3.00	20.00%	7.51%	0.23	1.00	98.00%	1.12	1,278	4,169	5,150	2879	4392	OK item
A	3.43	20.00%	10.36%	0.23	1.00	98.00%	1.12	1,209	4,345	5,465	2713	1584	Replenish inventory

Planners are often told to keep the master data parameters up to date by finding issues and then transferring the values to the master data team for adjustment. Companies generally have no problem understanding the need to have effective planning systems, but often miss the fact that they also need applications to enable these planning parameters to be analyzed and updated, and that they need to provide an effective way for those that have this responsibility to do so.

Barloworld's applications provide the following capabilities:

1. Allows planners to view the overall supply network.

2. Notifies planners about what to focus their attention on.

3. Allows the planners to manipulate supply planning parameters.

4. Provides planners with an understanding of the relationship between different supply planning elements.

A number of Barloworld's screens are examples of what I am referring to when I describe supply chain visibility. The following view highlights the obvious areas to be addressed by the planner. The categories F, M, and N on the next page are carrying far too much inventory according to what the Barloworld model recommends. Armed with this information, the planner can then go into the necessary details to determine why this is the case and take corrective action.

Conclusion

Arriving at the right combination of supply planning methods requires a detailed study of all the requirements and data necessary to drive the method. Without that upfront effort and knowledge, a method can end up being selected and then simply be perpetuated because of the strong tendency not to change decisions after they have been made.

A major challenge of all application implementations is how to keep track of the settings in the application. Therefore, one of the most important steps to be performed during the implementation is to determine which fields should have values assigned to them by the business. In this chapter, I highlighted an approach which maintains many of the master data fields outside of the supply planning application.

Conclusion

Procedural versus Lean planning is one of the most enduring debates in the area of supply planning. Lean is a both a philosophy and a number of techniques. Lean adherents propose that the standard mathematics of everything from the standard supply and production planning methods to Economic Order Quantity are incorrect and can be improved upon by reducing order quantities.

Within Lean, there are actually a number of techniques, with reorder points being just one of them. The proposal of this book is that the strongest approach actually leverages both schools of thought. The trick is determining which segments of the product location database should go out on which school of thought.

A major difference between Lean and MRP, or more accurately Lean versus procedural-based supply and production planning primarily has to do with the replenishment trigger. Supply and production planning procedures such as MRP, heuristics, allocation, cost optimization and inventory optimization work off projections, while Lean replenishment works off an immediate need; at least this is most often the case, as there are some reorder points which calculate based upon projections.

Reorder points can be calculated a number of ways. For instance, they can be calculated differently based upon whether the **demand history is lumpy or stable**.

Lean adherents propose that the standard mathematics of everything from the standard supply and production planning methods to Economic Order Quantity are incorrect and can be improved upon by reducing order quantities. Lean proponents make accurate points that the way that MRP and other supply and production planning software is implemented and run in most companies leaves a significant opportunity for improvement.

It is also true that there is less than meets the eye with some of the most popular and well-known inventory calculations. For instance, EOQ often leaves out a number of considerations outside of ordering and holding costs. While there are many varieties of EOQ formulae that can be pulled from research papers, there is also considerable complexity involved in using these more advanced formulae. It is difficult to find a formula which incorporates all the dimensions of factors that should set the economic order quantity – and of course only the more basic EOQ formulae tend to be available in enterprise software.

The standard dynamic safety stock formula is also problematic and much less useful than generally proposed – as is covered in the SCM Focus Press book *Safety Stock and Service Levels: A New Approach*.

Reorder points are a major method used by proponents of Lean. Reorder point planning is an early approach to supply chain planning; however, while often dismissed as passé, it actually has applicability to a number of circumstances. Reorder point planning can be used effectively for products that are **both easy and difficult** to forecast.

What works well for products with erratic demand history works equally well for products with extremely stable demand history. Reorder points were the primary planning approach used by companies before MRP and DRP were developed and offered in software. However there are now many quite sophisticated reorder point formulae – although it is rare that anything but the basic reorder point formula finds its way into an enterprise software application.

A reorder point is very simply a quantity of stock or an interval at which a "reorder," or order, is to be created. In reorder point planning, orders are not triggered by a specific requirement (such as a forecast or dependent requirement), but instead by the depletion of stock over time, eventually triggering the minimum stock level or reorder point.

Reorder points can be used with any of the supply planning methods, or they can be used to exclusively control the supply plan **without any of the methods**. However, when they are used exclusively to control the supply plan, the company is **said to be performing** reorder point planning, as opposed to forecast-based planning. MRP/DRP and APS (heuristic, allocation, cost optimization, inventory optimization) methods are forecast-based planning.

A lot of energy is spent on debating between Lean and procedural planning. However, both camps tend to provide too little in the way of evidence for their claims. Coming up from the procedural school of thought, I was guilty of this myself. For some time, I believed that the standard inventory formulae were reliable – until I tested them in great detail and found flaws in their output, which depended upon the circumstance.

Instead of spending time in either of the camps, I would recommend testing both Lean and procedural planning techniques to see which are most appropriate for different product location combinations and then using whatever works. Without testing, it is too easy to simply fall back to whatever one's background is. However, through testing one can not only drive to the use of the best technique per circumstance, but also increases one's knowledge level. Most supply planning systems have both types of functionality available with them, therefore it is just a matter of knowing which type of functionality to apply to which product location combinations.

When Reorder Points are Forecast Based Replenishment

If one reads through any number of books on inventory management and supply planning, one will come across the following phrase in some shape or form:

"Reorder points are a non-forecast based method for supply planning."

I have made this statement several times in this book and, by and large, it is a reliable statement. However, SAP APO SNP changed the calculation method so that it calculates forward. With the reorder points in SAP ERP, it does not matter if you enter forecasts, because the SAP reorder points do not forward calculate.

However in SAP APO, as long as forecasts are entered, and because the reorder points in APO calculate on the basis of planned stock on hand (and not actual stock on hand), reorder point-based orders can be created for the entire planning horizon. This means that SAP has converted the reorder point to be a forecast based planning method.

This is demonstrated in a mockup of the SAP APO planning book (the main user interface for SAP DP and SAP SNP), which is included below:

Planning Book Mockup

	Key Figure Name	Common Order Categories	10/5/14	10/12/14	10/19/14
Demand	Forecast		5000	1000	300
	Sales Order		5500	0	0
	Unconsumed Forecast		0	1000	300
	Distribution Demand	Unconfirmed Purchase Requisition (either internal or external source of supply)			1200
	Distribution Demand Confirmed	Confirmed Purchase Requisitions or Purchase Orders			
	Dependent Demand				
	Total Demand		**5,500**	**1,000**	**1,500**
Supply	Distribution Receipt	Stock Transport or Purchase Requisition			200
	Distribution Receipt Confirmed	Stock Transport Orders and Purchase Orders			
	In Transit		500		
	Production Planned		2,800	600	1,300
	Production Confirmed				
	Total Receipts		**3,300**	**600**	**1,500**
Stock	Stock on Hand		1,000	600	600
	Max Stock Level		600	600	600
	Reorder Point		500	500	500
	Safety Stock		500	300	300

As you can see, this spreadsheet mockup simulates the forward calculating reorder point in SNP. While there are no sales orders after the first time bucket, there are forecasts in every time bucket, and this drives reorder point based planned orders into the future. I have also "set" a maximum stock quantity, so APO would therefore manage its planned orders to come in underneath this maximum stock level.

Inventory Parameter Calculation with 3S

I am such a proponent of integrated inventory parameter optimization that I have developed a software calculator that does just this. This calculator is called the *SCM Focus Service Level Scenario Setting and Parameter Optimizer* or 3S for short.

The Conceptual Underpinnings of 3S

3S is based upon three overarching concepts, which derive from having been in many company environments and considering the reality of how supply and production planning systems are used.

1. *Inventory Calculations:* 3S calculates its parameter output through applying formulas that are similar to standard formulae that can be found in inventory management books, but have been customized to provide more usable output. Unlike an academic paper, all of our formulae need to work together – and we found improvements that allow them to work together better. This leads to the next point.

2. *Constrained Parameters and Parameter Inputs:* The standard calculations tend to assume that the capacity at the company is unlimited. In order to obtain constraints, most companies

purchase an expensive system. However, we have found there are ways of constraining parameter inputs that are more straightforward. In fact, one of the most interesting opportunities is the ability to use 3S to constrain systems that do not have constraints – and this is the vast majority of supply and production planning systems in use today.

3. *Global View:* 3S calculates individual values, but looks at the overall product location database to do so. This means that the individual settings are congruent with the big picture.

The Process

3S requires data that is available from most companies, but we have to format it to work with the 3S calculations. For instance, 3S does not calculate safety stock or several other values by using the normal forecast error and supply lead-time variability measurements. This means that we work with clients to access the input data and then we format it ourselves.

Companies have similarities in their parameter needs, but they also have differences. We have standard calculations as part of 3S - but we also have the ability to adjust some of the calculations for specific customer requirements. We don't yet have the process down as a template and consider the customization part to be important and something we are more comfortable assuring quality if we do ourselves.

How S3 Output Is Updated

3S is **not an online** application, but is a **periodically-run** application, and therefore it is very efficient for clients to re-engage us and faster for us to run the application and then provide the output file – which can then be uploaded to the ERP system. This takes a load off of the planning function in the company.

Net Change Parameter Updating

Updating the service levels and parameters of a company does not mean processing all of the product location database again - instead I recommend selecting new products or products that have gone through a significant change, and processing those.

This type of **net change** processing can happen at any time, and updating the parameters is not an onsite project but is engaged in remotely and requires far fewer hours than the initial project. A segmentation of product/location combinations during a net change parameter update might look like the following.

More on 3S can be found at the 3S website at http://www.scmfocus.com/3S. In my view, an integrated parameter calculation of this type is the fastest as well as the least expensive way to improve the output of not only MRP, but all supply planning and production planning methods currently in use.

References

A Brief History of Just In Time. Strategos Inc.
http://www.strategosinc.com/just_in_time.htm

Byrnes, Jonathan. Islands of Profit in a Sea of Red Ink. Portfolio Hardcover.
2010.

Cargo Cult Science, Wikipedia June 11 2014
http://en.wikipedia.org/wiki/Cargo_cult_science

Castenllina, Nick. To ERP or Not to ERP: In Manufacturing, It Isn't Even a Question, Aberdeen. 2011
http://aberdeen.com/aberdeen-library/7116/RA-enterprise-resource-planning.aspx

Control Charts. Wikipedia. June 25 2014
http://en.wikipedia.org/wiki/Control_charts

Demand Works Smoothie Help, Version 7.3, 2013

Discrete Manufacturing. Wikipedia. October 23, 2013.
http://en.wikipedia.org/wiki/Discrete_manufacturing

Ford, Henry. Bakken, James K. Bodek, Norma. Crowther, Samuel. Today and Tomorrow. Productivity Press. December 1988.

Harris. Ford W. How Many Parts to Make at Once. Factory, The Magazine of Management. 1913.

Johnson, Giles. Making MRP Work: A Practical Guide to Improving Your System's Performance. Smartspeed Consulting Limted. 2013.

Lean Manufacturing. Wikipedia, June 17 2014

http://en.wikipedia.org/wiki/Lean_manufacturing

Lingus, Richard G. The Rise and Fall or MRP. Rockford Consulting. 1991.

http://rockfordconsulting.com/the-rise-and-fall-of-mrp.htm

MRP. Accessed October 18, 2013. http://en.wikipedia.org/wiki/Material_requirements_planning

Ohno, Taiichi. Bodek, Norman. Toyota Production System: Beyond Large Scale Production. Productivity Press. 1988.

Plossl, George. Production and Inventory Control: Principles and Techniques. 2nd ed. Prentice Hall, 1985.

Plossl, George. Orlicky's Material Requirement's Planning. Second Edition. McGraw Hill. 1984. (first edition 1975)

Reorder point, Wikipedia, January 10 2012. http://en.wikipedia.org/wiki/

Reorder_point

Silver, Edward A. Peterson, Rein. Decision Systems for Inventory Management and Production Planning. Second Edition. John Wiley and Sons. 1985.

Sievers, David, Hanna Hamburger, and Julie Bonne. *Uncovering the Hidden Costs of Trade Promotions.* Sales and Marketing Management, July 31, 2010.

http://www.salesandmarketing.com/article/uncovering-hidden-costs-trade-promotions.

Smith, Chad. Ptak, Carol. Orlicky's Material Requirements Planning (3rd Edition) McGraw-Hill Professional. May 11, 2011.

Snapp, Shaun. Process Industry Manufacturing Software. SCM Focus Press. 2013.

Snapp, Shaun. Safety Stock and Service Levels: A New Approach. SCM Focus Press. 2015.

Snapp, Shaun. Supply Planning with MRP, DRP and APS Software. SCM Focus Press. 2013.

Snapp, Shaun. Repairing Your MRP System. SCM Focus Press. 2015.

Snapp, Shaun. Multi Method Supply Planning in SAP APO. SCM Focus Press. 2013.

Snapp, Shaun. Promotions Forecasting: Techniques of Forecast Adjustments in Software. SCM Focus Press. 2015.

Smoothie Help Documentation, 2010, Demand Works.

Sobek III, Durward K. Smalley, Art. Understanding A3 Thinking: A Critical Component of Toyota's PDCA Management System. Productivity Press. 2008.

Toyoda Kiichiro, Wikipedia. June 17 2014.

http://en.wikipedia.org/wiki/Kiichiro_Toyoda

Waddell, Bill. "MRP vs. Lean." Evolving Excellence Blog. Last modified May 27, 2006.

http://www.evolvingexcellence.com/blog/2006/05/mrp_versus_Lean.html.

Ward, J. B. "Determining Reorder Point When Demand is Lumpy," Management Science, 1978.

What is MRP (I,II) Full citation lacking, but available at this link

http://www.share-pdf.com/73ec30f31e4e41e29f089357308d2349/What%20is%20MRP.pdf

http://www.sciencedirect.com/science/article/pii/0272696381900310

What is MRP: Software Material Requirements Planning Software Explained

http://blog.e2banytime.com/what-is-mrp-software-material-requirements-planning-software-explained/

Wight, Oliver. The Oliver Wight Class A Checklist for Business Excellence. Sixth Edition. Oliver Wight International. 2005

http://help.sap.com/saphelp_40b/helpdata/en/7d/c27102454011d182b40000e829fbfe/content.htm

http://help.sap.com/saphelp_40b/helpdata/en/7d/c2711c454011d182b40000e829fbfe/content.htm

http://help.sap.com/saphelp_erp60_sp/helpdata/en/f4/7d257044af11d182b40000e-829fbfe/frameset.htm

Vendor Acknowledgments and Profiles

I have listed brief profiles of each vendor with screen shots included in this book below.

Profiles:

SAP
SAP does not need much of an introduction. They are the largest vendor of enterprise software applications for supply chain management. SAP has multiple products that are showcased in this book, including SAP ERP and SAP APO.

www.sap.com

Demand Works
Demand Works is a best-of-breed demand-and-supply-planning vendor that emphasizes flexible and easy-to-configure solutions. This book only focuses on the supply planning functionality within their Smoothie product, which includes MRP and DRP.

http://www.demandworks.com

Barloworld

Barloworld has 350 customers for its supply chain planning and network planning tools, covering such industries as automotive, industrial, retail, wholesale and distribution. The supply chain planning product set offers a focused supply chain planning footprint.

www.barloworld.com

Author Profile

Shaun Snapp is the founder and editor of SCM Focus. SCM Focus is one of the largest independent
supply chain software analysis and educational
sites on the Internet.

After working at several of the largest consulting
companies and at i2 Technologies, he became an
independent consultant and later started SCM Focus. He maintains a strong interest in comparative
software design, and works both in SAP APO as
well as with a variety of best-of-breed supply chain
planning vendors. His ongoing relationships with these vendors
keep him on the cutting edge of emerging technology.

Primary Sources of Information and Writing Topics

Shaun writes about topics with which he has firsthand experience.
These topics range from recovering problematic implementations,
to system configuration, to socializing complex software and supply
chain concepts in the areas of demand planning, supply planning
and production planning.

More broadly, he writes on topics supportive of these applications, which include master data parameter management, integration, analytics, simulation and bill of material management systems. He covers management aspects of enterprise software ranging from software policy to handling consulting partners on SAP projects.

Shaun writes from an implementer's perspective and as a result he focuses on how software is actually used in practice rather than its hypothetical or "pure release note capabilities." Unlike many authors in enterprise software who keep their distance from discussing the realities of software implementation, he writes both on the problems as well as the successes of his software use. This gives him a distinctive voice in the field.

Secondary Sources of Information

In addition to project experience, Shaun's interest in academic literature is a secondary source of information for his books and articles. Intrigued with the historical perspective of supply chain software, much of his writing is influenced by his readings and research into how different categories of supply chain software developed, evolved, and finally became broadly used over time.

Covering the Latest Software Developments

Shaun is focused on supply chain software selections and implementation improvement through writing and consulting, bringing companies some of the newest technologies and methods. Some of the software developments that Shaun showcases at SCM Focus and in books at SCM Focus Press have yet to reach widespread adoption.

Education

Shaun has an undergraduate degree in business from the University of Hawaii, a Master of Science in Maritime Management from the Maine Maritime Academy and a Master of Science in Business Logistics from Penn State University. He has taught both logistics and SAP software.

Software Certifications

Shaun has been trained and/or certified in products from i2 Technologies, Servigistics, ToolsGroup and SAP (SD, DP, SNP, SPP, EWM).

Contact

Shaun can be contacted at: shaunsnapp@scmfocus.com

Abbreviations

APO – Advanced Planner and Optimizer
APS – Advanced Planning and Scheduling
BOM – Bill of Materials
CPG – Consumer Packaged Goods
CTM – Capable to Match
DRP - Distribution Requirements Planning
EOQ – Economic Order Quantity
ERP – Enterprise Resource Planning
JIT – Just in Time
MRP– Material Requirements Planning
MPS – Master Production Schedule
PLC – Product Location Combination
ROQ – Reorder Quantity
SNP – Supply Network Planning
TSL – Target Stock Level
S&OP – Sales and Operations Planning
TPS – Toyota Production System
WIP – Work in Process
3S – Service Level Scenario Setter and Parameter Optimizer

Links Listed in the Book by Chapter

Chapter 1:

http://www.scmfocus.com/supplyplanning/2011/10/02/the-four-factors- that-make-up-the-master-production-schedule/

http://www.scmfocus.com/supplyplanning/2014/04/09/dynamic-reorder-point-calculator/

http://www.scmfocus.com/writing-rules/

http://www.scmfocus.com

http://www.scmfocus.com/supplyplanning

Chapter 4:

http://www.scmfocus.com/supplyplanning/2014/04/20/economic-order-quantity-calculator-pull-forward-inventory-build/

Chapter 5:

http://www.scmfocus.com/supplychaincollaboration/2012/02/lean-as-acover-story-by-oems-to-force-their-poor-planning-decisions-on-contractmanufacturers/

http://www.youtube.com/watch?v=V5e1YKkZFhc

Chapter 7:

Hagemeyer,Dale. *Vendor Panorama for Trade Promotion Management in Consumer Goods.* Gartner, 2012.

Lucas, Anthony. "In-Store Trade Promotions – Profit or Loss?" *Journal of Consumer Marketing.* April 1, 1996.

Appendix A

http://www.scmfocus.com/3S

www.ingramcontent.com/pod-product-compliance
Lightning Source LLC
LaVergne TN
LVHW080100070326
832902LV00014B/2332